PREMARITAL GUIDANCE

CREATIVE PASTORAL CARE AND COUNSELING

PREMARITAL GUIDANCE

Charles W. Taylor

FORTRESS PRESS　　　　　　MINNEAPOLIS

PREMARITAL GUIDANCE

Cover design: Brad Norr
Cover photograph: copyright © 1998 PhotoDisc, Inc.

Library of Congress Cataloging-in-Publication Data

Taylor, Charles W., date
    Premarital guidance / Charles W. Taylor.
        p.   cm. — (Creative pastoral care and counseling series)
    Includes bibliographical references (p.   ).
    ISBN 0-8006-2712-1
    1. Marriage counseling. 2. Pastoral counseling. 3. Marriage — Religious aspects — Christianity. I. Title. II. Series.
BV4012.27.T38   1999
259'.13 — dc21   98-43461
                                                                          CIP

The paper used in this publication meets the minimum requirements of American National Standard for Information Sciences—Permanence of Paper for Printed Library Materials, ANSI Z329.48-1984.

Manufactured in the U.S.A.   AF 1-2712

03   02   01   00   99   1   2   3   4   5   6   7   8   9   10

To my wife, Marlene L. Jones Taylor

CONTENTS

EDITOR'S FOREWORD

Have you ever wondered why so few books are written on premarital guidance? Why this key pastoral task is rarely discussed at seminary training or continuing education events? One might wonder if this dearth of information covers the embarrassment of clergy who have marriages go up in smoke a few years later.

In *Premarital Guidance*, Charles Taylor does not rehash well-worn phrases about marriage. He combines systems theory, cognitive therapy, sociological data, and the traditions of the church with pastoral theology and pastoral care into a useful book that views premarital guidance from a new and fresh perspective. He extends the metanoia model, which he developed previously in *The Skilled Pastor*, to the premarriage preparations pastors do. This approach brings together a couple's issues and tasks with a pastor's resources.

The author wisely shies away from the term "premarital pastoral counseling" and instead refers to the task as "premarital guidance." Premarital guidance, he points out, includes a wide variety of ministries to the couple—certainly broader than classic pastoral counseling.

In Chapter 1 Taylor details four aspects of premarital guidance: religious marital preparation, couple issues and tasks, pastoral resources, and the bringing together of the couple's issues and tasks with the pastor's resources. Chapter 2 describes the skills clergy need to be helpful to couples preparing for marriage. Chapter 3 discusses the specific components of premarital sessions, topics that need addressing in the opening session and in subsequent sessions. In Chapter 4 Taylor presents and discusses what he believes are the three fundamental tasks of the journey into marriage—getting a blessing, leaving, and cleaving.

Chapter 5 focuses on relating scripture to the couple's issues and tasks. Here Taylor looks at marriage from a theological standpoint. Much of the chapter centers on developing an understanding of Ephesians 5:21-33. (Since this is probably the most important New Testament text on marriage, it is a critical one for pastors to consider and use in their premarital ministry.) Chapter 6 deals with helping the couple plan their wedding. In it Taylor describes *elicitive teaching* as a way to help couples reflect on their families of origin as well as on their theological understanding of marriage. The book ends with very useful appendixes that make recommendations concerning the structure of interviews, useful couples workbooks, premarital inventories, marriage preparation courses, and prayers for the marriage.

Premarital Guidance is solid in both theory and practice. Taylor weaves together family systems theory and pastoral theological reflection. It is also an eminently practical book, offering numerous suggestions for carrying out a ministry of premarital care in parish settings. It is my hope that *Premarital Guidance* will challenge you, the reader, to look more closely at the task of marital preparation, and that your ministry will enhance the life journey of each newly joined couple in your congregation.

HOWARD W. STONE

ACKNOWLEDGMENTS

I must begin by thanking the Rev. Kenneth D. Higgenbotham, who first showed me the power and importance of premarital preparation. Next let me express appreciation for the Rev. Dr. Bonnie Ring, who was my partner in developing and teaching a workshop on premarital guidance for the Diocese of Montana during which we presented many of the ideas about premarital guidance that are found in this book. Certainly the Bishop and clergy of the Diocese of Montana must also be recognized for getting me started. To be commended, also, are those who attended my subsequent workshops on premarital guidance, during which many ideas were refined. Many accolades go to Church Divinity School of the Pacific professors Arthur Holder and Jane Menten for reading and making sage comments about early versions of the introduction and the first four chapters. Penultimately, I am grateful for Marlene, my wife. We fell in love, courted, attended premarital counseling, and married during the development of this book. This relationship, with all of its ups and downs, has immeasurably enriched this book. Above all I give praise to God on this Feast Day of St. Michael and All Angels (September 29) for all the angels that have protected me when the dragon and his angels sought to devour me and the book.

INTRODUCTION

How should pastors understand their ministry to premarital couples? Whom should pastors prepare for marriage? What should their goals be? Which resources should they use? *Premarital Guidance* responds to these questions by presenting a new model of premarital counseling. This model integrates helping skills with secular and religious resources to assist couples in dealing with the issues that marriage raises. It affirms the pastor's role by making religious teaching and wedding planning integral parts of premarital care.

This introductory chapter begins the task of responding to the type of questions that pastors ask. It sets the context for considering these concerns by introducing the two couples and their respective pastors who continue as illustrations throughout the book and illuminates these queries further by a discussion of the term *premarital guidance.*

BILL, SARAH, AND FR. SAM

Bill and Sarah came to the Rev. Sam Johnson's study at St. Paul's Episcopal Church for their first premarital session. Bill, a twenty-eight-year-old thin, blue-eyed blonde, stands six feet tall. He came to the session conservatively dressed in a tan tweed jacket, white dress shirt open at the neck, dark brown slacks, and brown "penny loafers." On his face he had a quiet, thoughtful expression, occasionally broken by a smile on his lips. Sam knew him slightly because Bill occasionally joined his mother, Susan, at Sunday morning services. Rev. Johnson was struck by the appearance of Bill's fiancée, Sarah, 25, a five-feet two-inch full figured brunette with flashing dark eyes and a smile bright enough to light up a small city, and intrigued by her decision to wear a bright red dress and high-heeled red pumps to this meeting.

Noting the significant differences in both their style of clothes and the way they presented themselves, the pastor speculated that these Caucasian partners were very different in personality and interests. He also noted the significant differences in their body types, hair color, and skin coloration and wondered if they came from different ethnic groups. Rev. Johnson wondered how these differences would surface and how he would respond to them.

With the recent divorces of two of the nicest couples he had worked with, Rev. Sam Johnson had the gnawing feeling that all the work he did with couples really didn't make any difference. The fact that so few of the couples he prepared for marriage ever joined his church also disillusioned him. Over time he realized that he had more than a few questions about premarital counseling; this part of his ministry frustrated him. As an attempt at revitalizing his premarital work, he had recently attended a workshop on premarital counseling. He wanted to test out with this couple some of the things that had been proposed at this workshop.

Forty-two-year-old Sam Johnson, an average-sized man with a medium build, stands about five feet nine inches tall. A blue-eyed brunette with a roundish face, Sam has a permanently pleasant but distant expression. Rev. Johnson's parishioners refer to him as Fr. Sam. This European-American pastor and his predominantly Caucasian congregation both feel comfortable with this combination of professional title and first name. Though a veteran with fifteen years' experience as a pastor, his ministry to premarital couples still makes Fr. Sam uneasy.

As Fr. Sam looked at Sarah and Bill, he wondered whether they would take premarital counseling seriously or just go through the motions like so many couples did. He feared the political bind he would be in if he refused to marry Bill and Sarah. Susan, the groom's mother, wielded a lot of power in St. Paul's Church because of her outgoing personality and her years of tireless involvement in church activities. Sam wondered if Bill or Sarah had a real interest in a Christian marriage or if they just wanted a wedding in a pretty church. Fr. Sam guessed that Bill came because Susan pressured him to get married in church. He often worried that his approach to premarital counseling did not meet the needs of unchurched couples or those not active in church.

RICH, WILMA, AND DR. WASHINGTON

When Rich, 36, and Wilma, 34—both divorced—came to Dr. Claretta Washington's study at Greater Mount Zion Baptist Church (GMZ), she expected that their marital preparation would be complex. She knew both of them: Wilma, a five-feet seven-inch trim, attractive, dark-brown-skinned woman with a long oval face that usually held a quiet smile, and Rich, her five-feet nine-inch, pudgy, and handsome fiancé, who had a square brown face that usually bore a reserved but intense expression. Wilma, who came to the interview in a gray double-breasted business suit with black low-heeled pumps had become a member of GMZ after her divorce three years ago. She and her two daughters had been regular participants in this large African-American congregation. Rich was nattily attired in a light-gray double-breasted herringbone suit with a white shirt, colorful tie, and dressy, black tasseled loafers. He had started coming to GMZ with Wilma a year ago.

Dr. Washington noticed that though both seemed somewhat happy, neither had that silly grin that she usually saw on the faces of engaged couples. On that basis, she wondered whether special problems caused their lack of giddiness and whether their previous marriages were a factor in their demeanor. She also surmised from their similar attire and expressions that this African-American couple had comparable tastes and personalities.

Claretta Washington, 53, whose skin has the color of rich coffee, stood five feet four, with a stocky frame. Her round face has a warm, accepting smile, and houses alert, playful eyes. The African-American congregation of GMZ, still responding to those Southern whites of previous generations who demeaned black elders and professionals by calling them by their first names, proudly call her Dr. Washington. This African-American woman feels very comfortable with this custom. Ordained seven years, Dr. Washington got her D. Min. in pastoral counseling soon after seminary and worked as a pastoral psychotherapist for three years before becoming the Minister for Families at GMZ a year ago.

Because of her training as a therapist, she could recognize the seriousness of the issues that Rich and Wilma brought as a couple remarrying. She wondered how she should deal with them as part of a local church pastoral staff. Their presence caused her to revisit the questions that she brought to premarital counseling: How do I use my counseling skills in a way that witnesses to the gospel? How can I use Scripture and prayer to help couples? Now that I am a local church pastor, should I refer couples that I would have counseled as a psychotherapist? These questions had led her to attend the same workshop on premarital ministry as Fr. Sam.

This book is written for persons like Fr. Sam and Dr. Washington who have questions about their participation in the church's ministry to couples preparing for marriage. Though it does not give definitive answers, this book does respond to these questions by raising important issues and making concrete suggestions. The book's first response to Fr. Sam, Dr. Washington, and others is the suggestion of a new term to replace premarital counseling.

GUIDANCE, NOT COUNSELING

This book calls the ministry to couples before marriage "premarital guidance" because the term *guidance* can include a variety of types of personal ministries, whereas the term *counseling* indicates intense problem solving or therapy. On the other hand, *guidance* has a broader meaning. Clebsch and Jaekle (1964) listed it as one of the four historical pastoral care functions. They defined it as "assisting perplexed persons to make confident choices between alternative courses of thought and action, when such choices are viewed as affecting the present and future state of the soul."

Clinebell (1984, 43) discusses contemporary forms of guidance as "intertwining education and counseling." Clinebell (1984, 34) also states that pastoral care "is the task of the whole congregation." I would add that participation in the activities of the congregation is an integral part of adult religious education.

Thus, the term *guidance* is broad enough to include the many ministries that pastors might provide to couples preparing to marry: giving counsel, educating, administrating, preparing and leading worship, involving lay couples in working with the couple, and referring couples to therapists.

The common name for the ministry of pastors or others to engaged couples is *premarital counseling*. Premarital conversations differ however, in several important ways, from the consultations that we normally call "counseling."

First, people come to counseling with an awareness that they have a problem, and the discussion is shaped by their admission of need. Premarital conferences, in contrast, are shaped by the fact that during the period before marriage, many couples are least aware of and least forthcoming about their problems.

Second, persons in need who are motivated to consider their issues usually initiate counseling; quite often church policy or the pastor require premarital meetings. Likewise, many couples come to pastors solely for cooperation in putting on the wedding.

The fact that many couples' primary motive for talking to pastors has to do with getting liturgical help at best or obtaining a religious person or setting to add to their wedding at worst defines a third characteristic that separates premarital discussions from ordinary counseling. The expectation of many denominations that the pastor will educate the couple about marriage constitutes a fourth factor that distinguishes premarital sessions from the more problem-solving or therapeutic aims typical of counseling.

For the four reasons discussed above, this book calls these premarital conversations "premarital guidance" rather than "counseling."

NEW NAME, NEW PERSPECTIVE

This discussion of terms has a very practical motivation: to help pastors conceive of the premarital ministry in a way that helps them to understand it better and enjoy it more.

Much of the discomfort that some pastors feel about their premarital ministry stems from their thinking of it as counseling. Some of their uneasiness comes from the differences between premarital ministry and counseling—the couple is not admitting their problems, they seem more interested in the wedding than the marriage, and there are pressures to teach about marriage. Another source of concern derives from the fact that pastors do not have the permission or therapeutic contract, from most couples, to do the counseling that may be needed. Many pastors' queasiness about premarital interviewing comes from their belief that they lack the counseling skills to give couples the help they need. Thus, three factors combine to make the term *premarital counseling* unhelpful: the differences between premarital guidance and counseling, the lack of a therapeutic contract, and the limited counseling skills of some pastors. Because of these concerns, pastors raise many questions out of their frustration with premarital counseling. Fr. Sam asks, "How do I have an in-depth discussion about marriage with a couple who is only interested in a wedding?" "How do I surface the most strategic issues for discussion?" "How can I turn this time into more than obligation?" Dr. Washington asks, "How can you teach about marriage and counsel at the same time?" "What does this premarital work have to do with my ministry as a religious leader?" "Do I refer those who really need counseling?" Both wonder, "How do I do a responsible job in the time I have to give to the couple or in the time the couple will give me?"

Calling the ministry to couples preparing for marriage "premarital guidance" helps pastors to appreciate and enhance the attractive features of this work. For example, these couples bring an optimistic attitude, a welcome change from the despair that drags people to "counseling." As "guidance," and therefore "a ministry rooted in a tradition of faith," premarital conferences and weddings become opportunities either to share the faith in depth with couples who practice the tradition, like Wilma and Rich, or to proclaim it afresh to non-practicing couples like Sarah and Bill.

Thinking of premarital ministry as guidance has two further benefits. First, it increases the number of resources that can be appropriately used. Counseling focuses on talk as the primary aid, whereas guidance leads pastors to think of other resources such as prayer, rites, religious groups, Scripture, and various lay (non-ordained, non-counselor) ministers. Second, the term *premarital guidance* can put this ministry in the proper perspective by viewing it as but one small part of the religious community's multifaceted and life-long program of care.

Considering marriage preparation as part of the church's ongoing ministry can remove some of the pressure to get all marriage preparation done in premarital sessions. When one considers this ministry in the context of the church's pastoral care, it makes sense that pastors should use every means possible to invite couples to continue the process of growing into marriage through participating in congregational life. There special marital enrichment events, as well as its regular worship, education, fellowship, and outreach, offer couples the religious experience, theological understanding, group support, and mission that they need for their marriages.

In sum, this book uses the term *premarital guidance* for the ministry to couples preparing for marriage. It uses this term as a way of incorporating the pastor's multifaceted role as liturgical leader, administrator, facilitator of ministries, spiritual guide, preacher, teacher, and evangelist into the ministry to the engaged. The following pages describe a process of premarital guidance that employs this complicated pastoral role in responding to couples' needs. Why name it "premarital guidance"? Because this new name points to a fresh perspective.

1

FOUR ASPECTS
OF PREMARITAL GUIDANCE

Premarital guidance involves bringing together couples' issues and tasks with pastoral resources for religious marriage preparation. This chapter presents the four key aspects of premarital guidance: religious marriage preparation, couples' issues and tasks, pastoral resources, and bringing together.

RELIGIOUS MARRIAGE PREPARATION

Religious marriage preparation involves education in the beliefs and practices presented in a religious wedding service. The concepts and rituals of the marriage rite constitute those that a denomination thinks are most instructive for couples beginning religious marriage. Churches recommend such religious marriage preparation in the belief that this training will prove beneficial to the couple in their marriage.

Religious marriage preparation is the goal of premarital guidance. The word *religious* makes this definition wide enough to fit pastoral guidance in various faiths, while also allowing for ministry to mixed-faith couples. For example, a Jewish man and a Christian woman could be prepared for a service that combines the two traditions and implies that each will live out its implications by practicing his or her own faith. The examples in this book are limited to Christian marriage, because of this author's lack of training and experience in preparing couples of other religions.

The various Christian denominational services and official commentaries make clear that their rites are designed for a religious (Christian) marriage. Those that recommend or require marriage preparation prescribe it as preparation for understanding Christian marriage. For example, Canon 18 Section 2 of the canons (official laws) of Fr. Sam's denomination, the Episcopal Church (Church 1991, 49–50), states in part:

> Before solemnizing a marriage, the Member of the Clergy shall have ascertained: . . . b) That both parties understand that Holy Matrimony is a physical and spiritual union of a man and a woman, entered within the community of faith, by mutual consent of heart, mind, and will, and with

the intent that it be lifelong. . . . d) That at least one of the parties has received Holy Baptism. e) That both parties have been instructed as to the nature, meaning and purpose of Holy Matrimony. . . .

By stating that Holy Matrimony is "entered within the community of faith," requiring that "at least one of the parties has received Holy Baptism," and requiring instruction "as to the nature, meaning and purpose of Holy Matrimony by the Member of the Clergy," the content of the canon clearly focuses on Christian religious marriage preparation.

The Goal of Christian Marriage Preparation

Fr. Sam brought questions about the goal of Christian marriage preparation to the workshop that he attended. He wanted to know how this goal applied to couples who appeared to be seeking only marriage in a church rather than Christian marriage preparation. He asked, "Why teach the religious understandings to them?"

At the workshop he learned that the religious understanding of marriage is offered to the couple for three important reasons. First, the desire for a church wedding or pastor's blessing on a marriage often contains an unarticulated request for the deeper experience of blessing offered by religious marriage. Couples come to a pastor because the church offers something special, even though they cannot define it, or they think it's about the magic of the minister or the building. Religious marriage preparation gives the couple an opportunity to participate more deeply in that "special blessing" they seek.

Second, religious preparation helps pastors clarify their ministry to those preparing for marriage. Once pastors accept religious marriage preparation as a goal, they know more about what they are trying to do and with whom they will do it. Thus, Fr. Sam's vague worries about Sarah and Bill's interest in Christian marriage can be replaced with a clarified relationship. Fr. Sam can explain his beliefs and invite them to explore religious preparation if they choose or to work with someone else if they choose. Clarity about religious preparation can reduce the amount of time spent wrestling with couples who have no intention of preparing for a religious marriage. More important, this clarity helps those couples who come vaguely intending Christian marriage to choose wholehearted preparation for it.

Third, the Christian community believes that religious understandings will sustain and deepen the joy of the couple, and that God wants for the couple what the couple wants, namely: mutual joy, and help and comfort in prosperity and adversity (cf. *Book of Common Prayer* 1979, 423). Its experience is that a relationship with God can expand mutual joy. Likewise, the reception of comfort from God in adversity increases the partners' ability to give comfort to each other and receive comfort from each other in adversity. This community assumes that regular participation in Christian worship and fellowship will help the couple develop the relationship with God that supports mutual joy and the mutual giving of comfort. Thus, Christians conclude that Christian marriage will enhance what the couple has and provide what they need. The church requires religious marriage preparation so that the couple can learn ways to get the blessing that they deeply want and that God wants them to have.

A Supporting Witness from Sociology

Though social-science study results can neither prove nor disprove theological claims, such research can provide support. Garland and Garland (1986, 8) report: "studies have found consistently that the most significant factor in the happiness of a marriage is 'religiosity,' a factor usually ignored and not even measured in most social science research." They cite Filsinger and Wilson's (1984) summary of research on predictors of marriage adjustment as support for this assertion.

Andrew Greeley's sociological research identifies the understanding of God and religious practices that contribute most to marital happiness. In the late 1970s Greeley did a study published as *The Young Catholic Family: Religious Images and Marriage Fulfillment* (1980). From a wide-ranging survey of young Roman Catholics he isolated the answers of 337 couples to one set of questions about their degree of marital satisfaction and sexual satisfaction and another set of responses to queries about frequency of prayer, type of religious beliefs, understandings of God, and church attendance. He then checked to see if there was a relationship between the two sets of answers. He discovered that high marital satisfaction and high sexual fulfillment were most frequently linked to praying daily, attending church weekly, and holding positive images of God. He also found that these positive images of God were deepened by listening to well-crafted sermons that emphasized God's love, attending prayer retreats, and doing devotional reading. Interestingly, those partners who both prayed daily (either alone or together) had a higher incidence of high marital satisfaction and high sexual fulfillment than any other group in this survey.

The discovery of the relationship between marital satisfaction and religious practice intrigued Greeley so much that he did a much larger study in the late 1980s, the results of which are published in *Faithful Attraction* (1991). In it he analyzed the results of two general surveys of the population of the United States and found that the most common characteristic of those who reported happy marriages was praying together. Prayer was more of a factor than income, education, or social class. Regular church attendance and frequent retreats devoted to prayer were also very common characteristics of those who reported happy marriages.

Greeley's research further revealed that those who prayed together often regularly scored higher on every other variable in this study: respect, trust, helping with household tasks, discussion of the state of the marriage, belief that the spouse is good with children, agreement on raising children, conviction that the spouse is a skilled lover, and frequent partying. Although identifying the reason or way that praying works to strengthen marriage is beyond the scope of sociological research, Greeley speculated that praying provides an interlude away from their other responsibilities in which couples "can share affection and common values and thus reinforce their relationship" (1991, 190).

Greeley's research cannot prove or even fully describe the power of prayer, worship, and good theology (warm images of God's love). Yet this witness seems to support the church's long-held wisdom that such pastoral resources are important for marriage. As Greeley writes, "Warm and intense images of God correlate with a warm and intense relationship with spouse" (1991, 193). Participating in worship and prayer and developing warm images of God's love are strongly correlated to what the engaged couple really wants—an enduring, fulfilling, transforming love. This promise motivates the church to offer religious preparation to those who seem not to be seeking a Christian marriage.

An Explanation from Psychology

An additional way of understanding why prayer, retreats, devotional reading, and well-crafted sermons help couples in their relationships comes from the Rational-Emotive Therapy (RET) developed by Albert Ellis (1962). This popular and effective approach emphasizes the centrality of beliefs in causing and maintaining human feelings and behaviors. RET maintains that because a person's beliefs about a situation contribute substantially to how he or she feels about the situation and responds to it, the way to change bad feelings and poor behaviors consists of changing unhelpful beliefs. Conversely, helpful beliefs sustain good feelings and behaviors.

RET practitioners use a variety of methods to dispute unhelpful beliefs and communicate helpful ones. They present helpful beliefs in workshops and weekly meetings through lectures, songs, and testimonies. Ellis and his disciples spread the word through popular books. RET therapists and RET self-help books encourage people to do daily mental imaging and meditative exercises on beliefs in order to change unhelpful beliefs to helpful beliefs. The methods RET practitioners use to communicate helpful beliefs and those they recommend to clients are similar to the activities Greeley found to be correlated to happy marriages. For example, mental imaging is similar to prayer; reading RET books is similar to devotional reading; and RET workshops or meetings with lectures, songs, and testimonies are similar to worship attendance.

Though Ellis maintains an antireligious stance, some religious writers have related the helpful beliefs to Christian beliefs. Paul A. Hauck correlated the helpful beliefs identified by Ellis with scriptural justification for teaching Self-Acceptance, the Unanxious Life, and Love and Forgiveness in *Reason in Pastoral Counseling* (1972). Building on Hauck's work, I reformulated Hauck's correlation and identified the helpful beliefs with the theological virtues of faith, hope, and love (Taylor 1991). This latter book discusses prayer, Scripture, rites, and other religious resources as ways of disputing unhelpful beliefs and communicating helpful ones.

RET and its Christian interpreters can help us understand the positive relationship between prayer and the related activities on the one hand and happy marriage on the other as follows: Prayer, along with prayer retreats, well-crafted sermons, devotional reading, and church attendance all communicate helpful beliefs and dispute unhelpful ones. It is these helpful beliefs that cause and sustain the good feelings and helpful behaviors that characterize happy marriages.

This cognitive explanation does not replace Greeley's more relational theory; it adds to it. Both relationship and belief are important. Thus, this book provides relationship skills and strategies for communicating helpful beliefs.

COUPLES' ISSUES AND TASKS

Couples bring many particular issues to the marriage preparation process. They introduce disagreements on personal styles, family training, and difficulties in communication and conflict resolution. Unhelpful beliefs that block resolution reside at the center of many of these disagreements. The pastoral resources of Scripture, the marriage rite, tradition, and theology can expose many unhelpful beliefs and suggest helpful ones.

Couples have three basic tasks as part of the marrying process: getting a blessing, leaving, and cleaving. After persons have chosen prospective mates and bonded with those persons to form intimate relationships, they want those relationships blessed—sanctified, celebrated, approved, and protected. The process of getting a blessing requires that persons leave or redefine their old relationships with families and friends in order to cleave to (cling to, join with) their mates.

As discussed in Chapter 4, these tasks have a religious core. Blessing is analogous to the experience of wholeness and transformation of which religious experience provides a foretaste. The tasks necessary to obtain the blessing—leaving and cleaving—are analogous to the leaving and cleaving that biblical figures such as Abraham, Moses, and Jesus did to obtain their blessings. Leaving is like a step of faith, and cleaving is like the Israelites' experience of bonding in the wilderness on the way to the Promised Land.

The combination of the religious nature of the tasks and the importance of helpful beliefs for happy feelings and good behaviors make religious marriage preparation very appropriate. The pastoral resources are not additions to marriage preparation but integral to it, because they help couples deal with the religious issues and beliefs that are at the core of their basic tasks as a couple.

PASTORAL RESOURCES

There are seven categories of religious or pastoral resources: the pastoral person, Scripture, Christian tradition, contemporary theology and ethics, covenant communities (groups of two or more persons who provide support for Christian living), prayer, and rites (Taylor 1991, 109–13). At least five of these resources are central to most religious marriage preparation: the pastoral person, Scripture, the marriage rite, prayer, and the pastor's congregation and groups (covenant community).

(1) Pastoral persons. Pastoral persons are the key resource for two reasons: (a) They represent God and the church and (b) they are responsible for communicating the gospel by introducing the couple to the other resources. Pastors are the gatekeepers to the religious resources.

The representative nature of the pastoral role means that pastor's self-awareness, relationships to family and congregation, knowledge of the resources and couples' tasks, and pastoral conversational skills are foundational parts of effective premarital guidance. Thus, it is most important that pastors do three things to prepare themselves as effective religious resources: (a) Work on their own marriage or intimate relationships, for these both train and inspire the pastor; (b) take care of themselves by not doing weddings or rehearsals on off days or nights unless these off times can be transferred to another day in the same week; (c) participate in continuing education about premarital guidance. Poorly trained, tired pastors who are not taking care of their own relationships seldom communicate the good news effectively to couples preparing for marriage.

(2) Scripture. Scripture is the foundational teaching tool in all Christian churches. It contains the basic statements and stories of the good news by which all other statements and stories are measured. Pastors can help couples by challenging their unhelpful beliefs and guiding them into Christian beliefs through the use of Scripture.

(3) The marriage rite. The marriage rite is an especially helpful teaching tool in churches with official wedding liturgies such as the Catholic, Episcopal, Lutheran, Methodist, Presbyterian, and United Church of Christ. Rites in these churches integrate considerable religious wisdom about marriage from Scripture, tradition, and contemporary theology and ethics. They are designed to help couples, congregations, and pastors learn and pray about marriage. Thus, these rites pull together all seven religious resources in a form that couples can use to learn about and begin a religious marriage. Involving couples in designing and rehearsing these rites provides a way of teaching this wisdom, thus challenging unhelpful beliefs and communicating helpful ones.

(4) Prayer. As Greeley's research indicated, prayer is an important resource for couples. Pastors can help couples by teaching them to pray during the period of marriage preparation. The Scriptures, hymn texts, statements, and prayers of the wedding service provide suitable material for meditative prayer during this time. This meditative prayer helps solidify helpful beliefs. Healthy prayer both develops a couple's relationship to God and sustains helpful beliefs.

(5) Congregation. The congregation, with its people, policies, and programs, can provide couples with the support they need for a religious marriage, and pastors with the help they need for a marriage ministry. Some examples of congregational support are: (a) married couples in the congregation who mentor engaged couples; (b) married couples in the congregation who join with engaged couples in marriage classes and workshops; (c) a congregational wedding or marriage policy that prescribes the regulations regarding premarital guidance, the wedding service, and couple costs and responsibilities; (d) a wedding coordinator or committee that helps couples and pastors in making wedding arrangements; (e) a committee or commission that supervises and supports premarital, neo-marital, and marriage enrichment ministries in the congregation.

In summary, the pastoral resources help the couple learn the helpful beliefs and develop the intimate relationship with God that are the twin foundations of a happy marriage.

BRINGING TOGETHER

Bringing together couple issues and tasks with pastoral resources is the central process of premarital guidance. This process can be understood by the use of the metanoia model (Taylor 1991, 8–11).

The Greek word *metanoia* means to change one's mind or attitude. This term, translated "repent," forms the center of Jesus' message: "The kingdom of God has come near; repent and believe in the good news" (Mark 1:15; cf. Matt. 4:17). Thus, the metanoia model emphasizes changing unhelpful understandings to Gospel beliefs as the way to help people.

The metanoia model recognizes three stages in dealing with an issue or need: (1) exploring the situation, (2) understanding the situation in terms of the gospel, and (3) acting appropriately. To aid parishioners in negotiating these stages, pastors use a specific group of skills to help in each stage: (a) *presence* or active listening skills to help parishioners explore the situation; (b) *proclamation* or assessing and challenging skills to help parishioners identify and challenge unhelpful understandings and adopt Gospel beliefs; and (c) *guidance* or planning skills to develop effective responses to the situation. Figure 1 below shows the relationships between the three stages and the three clusters of pastors' skills.

Fig 1: Pastor enables parishoner

SKILLS	STAGES
Presence	Exploring
Proclamation	Understanding
Guidance	Acting

In premarital work, couple tasks and pastoral resources are brought together. Pastors help couples *explore* their work on their issues and tasks, *understand* pastoral resources for coping with their concerns, and plan *actions* using their understandings. For example, during the earlier sessions of premarital care, pastors rely heavily on presence skills to help a couple talk about their relationship and their concerns. In later sessions pastors depend more on proclamation skills to foster the couple's understanding of their relationship and concerns in light of the gospel though pastoral resources such as Scripture, prayer, and rites. These later sessions also feature pastors' use of guidance skills as they aid the couple's plans for integrating their Gospel beliefs and the pastoral resources into the wedding, their relationship, and their individual lives.

This three-stage process of bringing together couple's tasks and pastoral resources responds to some of the concerns raised by the two pastors in the introduction. For example, Dr. Washington questioned how her counseling training would fit into premarital guidance. In the metanoia model, her therapeutic skills of providing a safe place would be invaluable in the exploring stage. Likewise, her ability to affirm the importance of conflict and to teach communication skills would help a couple to open up to her as pastor and to the wisdom of the Scriptures or wedding rite. Thus, her psychological training would prepare the way for the religious message.

Fr. Sam had wanted to know about the right process for couples who were Christian but not active church members and he also was concerned about teaching them religious understandings. The strategy of sharing the religious understandings in response to couples' needs gives these understandings a good opportunity to be understood as help rather than as an imposition. Because this method begins with the couple's needs rather than religious understandings, it is a good one to use with couples who are not active church members. It gives them a chance to test the usefulness of religious understandings in responding to their needs.

In sum, the process of bringing couples' issues and tasks together with pastoral resources forms the core of premarital guidance. This process follows the three stages of the metanoia model: exploring the couple's story, understanding it better, and planning action. Pastors emphasize specific skills in each stage: presence, proclamation, and guidance. This process and the skills needed for it are discussed in the rest of this book.

CONCLUSION

This chapter discusses four aspects of premarital guidance: religious marriage preparation, couples' issues and tasks, pastoral resources, and the process of bringing together the issues and the resources. By emphasizing the religious focus of premarital guidance, this discussion helps pastors both to relate this ministry to their other work and to decide with whom they will work. Identifying a couple's three basic premarital tasks as getting a blessing, leaving, and cleaving helps pastors understand the most important issues with which to deal. The discussion of the pastoral resources, especially pastor, Scripture, prayer, rites, and congregation, demonstrates the resources that pastors should use with couples preparing for marriage. Finally, the presentation of the process for bringing together pastoral resources and couple tasks, the metanoia model, indicates how one could teach about marriage and counsel at the same time. Thinking of premarital guidance as involving *bringing together couples' issues and tasks with pastoral resources for religious marriage preparation* provides a second major response to pastors' questions about ministry to engaged couples.

2

SKILLS FOR COUPLE CARE

How does one work with couples preparing for marriage? Which skills do pastors need to be helpful? What tactics are necessary? An illustrative opening session with Sarah, Bill, and Fr. Sam addresses these questions. The reflections on this session respond to these questions with some depth.

THE OPENING SESSION

Fr. Sam prepared for Bill and Sarah by placing two chairs fairly close together about six feet in front of the chair he would sit in. When Sarah and Bill came in and sat down, Sarah pulled her chair slightly forward and sat leaning forward. Bill did not move his chair forward, so he was slightly behind her, leaning back in his chair. Fr. Sam sat facing them, leaning slightly forward with his hands loosely on his knees. Immediately after the opening introductions, Sarah explained why they were there. "Father Johnson, we want to get married on September 18, and we want you to marry us. We think that your church is the perfect place for us; it's such a pretty place." Before Fr. Sam could respond, she went on to tell him about their wedding plans: They had rented the Spreemyer House (a local bed and breakfast place) for a reception; they were not having a sit-down meal or a band at the reception to save money; and they were keeping the guest list down to one hundred despite the large size of her family. She finished by saying, "The 18th is all right with you, isn't it? It is the perfect date for us." Fr. Sam looked at his calendar and saw that Saturday, September 18 was open, so he asked what time of day they would prefer. Sarah said two in the afternoon because she had always loved afternoon weddings. Fr. Sam told her he and the church were available at that time. Sarah leaned back a bit, having gotten her burning question answered.

When Sarah stopped talking, Fr. Sam took the opportunity to share his agenda for this opening session: (1) Discuss initial concerns, (2) spend a little time getting to know them, (3) explain how couples prepare for marriage at St. Paul's Episcopal Church, (4) get some basic information from them, (5) have them take a couples inventory. After a brief explanation of each item, Fr. Sam asked, "Is that agenda OK with each of you?" After they each gave approval, he then addressed Bill. "Since Sarah asked her question about the availability of the date, do you have a question, Bill?"

Bill sat up some and responded, "Is there a fee for using the church? My mother and I are long-term members, you know." Fr. Sam told Bill that because of janitorial fees and the increased use of lighting and heat there was a $100 fee, adding, "even for the family of a member who has worked as hard as Bill's mother." Bill then asked if that charge included the fee for the minister. Fr. Sam told him that the fee was just for the building. He added that he did not charge for his services, but that couples usually contributed to his discretionary fund (a fund used to help those with emergency needs) as a token of their gratitude. When Bill asked how much people normally gave, Fr. Sam told him that it ranged from $100 from some couples to several thousand from couples who gave a tithe (10 percent) of their wedding expenses. After responding to Bill's request to explain about tithing wedding expenses, Fr. Sam reminded Bill that what they give is up to them. Bill agreed to these terms, and then, satisfied that the key business arrangements were made, he leaned back and indicated that he was ready to move to the next item on the agenda.

Exploring Their Understandings: How Did You Decide to Marry?

Fr. Sam began the process of getting to know the couple by asking, "How did you decide to get married?" Sarah began giving the history of the relationship. She described how they met through a mutual friend, how they started off slowly because they were so different, how she began to feel that he was something special after a few months, and how she stopped dating anyone else. Bill chimed in, "I thought you were something special went I first saw you and dropped everyone else right then."

Sarah went on talking about their dating exclusively for a while and then, when her roommate left, their decision that the two of them would live together. Then her voice became a bit softer and her eyes misted and she said that one night when they had gone out to dinner, after they had been living together about seven months, Bill had gotten down on his knees in the restaurant and proposed. He had asked, "Will you marry me? I can't live without you!" Sarah went on, "That was so sweet, so romantic, and so unlike Bill, I just couldn't say no." Bill said quietly, "I have my moments."

Sarah concluded by saying, "My friends have been so excited that we are getting married; they just love Bill, even though he is quieter and more intellectual than they are." Bill added, "My mother and buddies love Sarah, too. She is the life of the party; she is really something special."

Fr. Sam looked at Bill and asked, "How would you tell the story of how the two of you decided to get married?" Bill replied, "I would tell it pretty much the same way as Sarah did, but I would add that I was amazed that the life of the party like Sarah would be attracted to a quiet guy like me. And when I saw how well we got along, I decided that I'd better pop the question before someone else did." Sarah, smiling broadly, said, "There was no one else, silly; but I am glad you asked."

Fr. Sam then said slowly, "The way I understand what you are saying is that even though you noticed at first that you were very different, you started dating and decided to live together after a while." "When my roommate left," Sarah interjected. "And then," continued Fr. Sam, "after about seven months, Bill proposed on his knees in a restaurant [Bill: "That's right"] and Sarah was really moved by this romantic gesture [Sarah: "You bet I was"]. What highlights did I miss?" "Good job, Father!" Sarah exclaimed, and Bill nodded affirmatively.

Fr. Sam now addressed Bill. "You both feel good about the fact that you are very different." After a brief hesitation, Bill said, "Yes, Sarah is the life-of-the-party type and I am the quiet type, [then speaking more rapidly] but we complement each other. I am helping her to think things out better and she is helping me to get out more." Turning to Sarah, Fr. Sam asked, "How would you talk about it?" Sarah began, "Yes, I am learning a lot from Bill, and it's remarkable how much he has come alive in the last few months. I am sure he is much happier. As Bill said, we help each other out, don't we, dear?" Bill smiled and shook his head up and down.

Fr. Sam offered a summary. "You are saying that your being different has been a help to each other and a positive thing, and you both feel very good about it." "It sure has," Bill responded immediately. "Yes, it's really changed my life." "And as Bill said, it's made our relationship really something," added Sarah. Fr. Sam wanted to pursue this point more, but he remembered that this couple was just getting to know him, so he held back. Then he ended the discussion of the first question by thanking them for helping him to get to know them by sharing about how they decided to get married.

Exploring Their Understandings: Why a Church Marriage?

With his first question answered, Fr. Sam popped the second: "Why do you want to get married in church?" From their expressions, Fr. Sam could tell that they were taken aback by the question. After what seemed like a long time, Sarah said, "I want a church wedding because it wouldn't seem like a real wedding if it wasn't in church." Bill chimed in, "That's right. Having a church wedding shows that you are serious about it, making your vows in front of God and everybody." After further discussion, Fr. Sam learned that Sarah was a Roman Catholic, and that although she was not a practicing Catholic, she still could not imagine a marriage that was not blessed in church. Neither could Bill, though he was not a very active member of St. Paul's. Both of these well-educated and articulate persons fumbled for words as they tried to explain what a church wedding meant, but they were both convinced that they needed one.

Fr. Sam continued by asking them if there were any other reasons that they wanted to be married in church. They both admitted that their parents really wanted them to be married in church. Sarah's Catholic parents were particularly insistent that this relationship be regularized by a church marriage. Bill's mother was also pushing him to tie the knot properly—that is, in church.

Fr. Sam summarized the conversation by asking, "Am I hearing you say that a church wedding gives a special blessing to a marriage, and you and your parents want that blessing for your marriage?" Bill gestured agreement, and Sarah said, "That's it, that's exactly what we have been saying, a church wedding gives the marriage a special blessing." Bill added, "We have a very special relationship and it deserves proper recognition."

Fr. Sam moved on to elicit their understandings of blessing by asking, "What do you want this special blessing to do for your relationship?" After a long, reflective silence, Bill spoke: "It gives our families and friends a chance to focus all their good thoughts, or you would say prayers, in support of our relationship. I am sure that all their support will help us." Sarah, chiding him with a smile, added, "Don't forget that we will be getting God's blessing, too. Isn't that the real reason for a church wedding, dear? As Mom always said, 'God's blessing makes the marriage holy and God will protect it because it is holy.'" Bill mumbled agreement, though he seemed a bit uncomfortable with Sarah's theology. He then added, "I think a lot of the blessing comes from our public dedication of ourselves to each other."

Though there was plenty of material to explore further, Fr. Sam decided that during this opening session he would just summarize what the couple said. "As I understand you, you are saying that the special blessing that you seek from a church wedding includes the supportive thoughts of your friends at the wedding, the blessing and protection of God for your marriage, and the power of your public dedication. Is that about it?"

"Yes," Bill said, "Yes, that's it." Sarah went on: "What about giving thanks for each other before God? That's a blessing, too—just like we used to give thanks before eating and call that a blessing." "A very good point, Sarah," Fr. Sam responded. "Giving thanks before God for each other is part of the special blessing of a church wedding. Are there any other points about the special blessing?" Sarah and Bill looked at each other and shook their heads. Fr. Sam concluded, "A church wedding is very important to you because it provides a special blessing in several different ways."

Negotiating the Contract

Fr. Sam moved to the third item on the agenda by saying, "Now that I have gotten to know you a little bit better, let me tell you how we prepare couples for marriage at St. Paul's. Bill, as you may know, the Episcopal Church requires that couples be prepared for marriage. After working with engaged couples for the fifteen years of my ministry and taking refresher courses on premarital counseling, I have developed a policy of meeting with couples at least six times before the wedding. Today is the first meeting. After this opening session I meet with couples at least three times to discuss issues in their relationship and twice to work on planning the wedding in light of those issues. In addition to these six sessions are the required wedding rehearsal and two dinner meetings with a couple from the parish. How does that sound to you?"

Bill and Sarah looked at each other, having been caught off guard by the prospect of six sessions. Then Sarah said, "Father, we have been living together for almost a year, and we get along really well. So we are not like some couples who don't really know each other and need a lot of help. Do we really have to go through all of this?"

Fr. Sam suppressed his urge to reply and asked, "What do you think, Bill?" Bill looked at Sarah, and then said, "Mom told me that there would be some sort of preparation to go through, but I didn't think it would be that much. I have been going to weddings all my life, and there is not that much to them that it would take two sessions to plan one. And as Sarah said, we are doing well together. We are pretty busy right now. Do you think all those sessions are really necessary?"

Fr. Sam wanted to shout something like, "You are too busy to spend a lousy six sessions preparing for a lifetime?" Instead he paraphrased their concerns: "You wonder if six sessions are necessary because you know each other pretty well and the service seems simple." When Bill and Sarah nodded affirmatively, Fr. Sam continued, "It's been my experience that couples have issues to work through no matter how long or how intensely they have known each other. I have worked with a lot of couples who have lived together one, two, or three years before preparing to get married, and they all found that they had issues to discuss. Are you willing to commit time to test that out?" Sarah looked at Bill, who said, "Of course we will do it if we have to." Fr. Sam decided to affirm even this begrudging agreement. "I am glad you are willing to try it, and I look forward to seeing if you have the same experience as others have had."

Fr. Sam continued, "Bill, I agree that the wedding services don't look like much to plan, but applying it to your issues takes the time. As you both said a few minutes ago, you want a church wedding because it gives a special blessing. Well, we have six sessions to help you get that blessing. The blessing is not just magic, though there is magic about weddings. A lot of the blessing comes through hard work, like facing your issues as preparation for the wedding, so that you can really say the vows knowing what you mean and they mean. Part of that blessing comes from your knowing what the service means, how it applies to you and your issues. Part of the blessing happens in relation to you and the wedding party being well-practiced and knowing what you are doing during the service. In fact, couples that I have prepared consistently tell me that the amount of preparation that they did helped their wedding to be extra special because they knew what they were doing. It takes a lot of work to fully participate in the special blessing of a church wedding. Are you willing to commit to this?"

Sarah and Bill looked at each other, and he answered, "Well, Father, I hadn't thought of it that way. It seems like there is a lot more to it than we had considered. But we are ready to try it, aren't we, Sarah?" "Yes, we certainly are!" she exclaimed. Fr. Sam concluded this part of the agenda by setting dates for the five upcoming sessions.

Getting the Basic Information

Fr. Sam then pulled out his information form for engaged couples and began to fill it out. He asked them for their full names, dates of birth, home and e-mail addresses, work and home phone numbers, pager and fax numbers, church affiliations, baptismal and confirmation dates, previous marriages (if any), dates of divorce or death of previous spouses (if any), name and ages of children, and so forth. After about ten minutes of asking these types of questions, and recording the information, the basics were established.

Introducing the Inventory

With the contract negotiated, Fr. Sam moved on to introduce the Prepare Inventory. He assured Sarah and Bill that their answers would be confidential, showed them how to fill out the information at the beginning, and then showed them how to mark their responses to the 165 questions of this computer-scored questionnaire. After telling them that it would take about thirty minutes to complete, Fr. Sam took each of them to a separate room to complete the questions. When they had finished, he debriefed them about the experience of completing the inventory. After reminding them of their appointment to meet in two weeks to review the results, he told them that they were free to discuss their responses with each other, and then bade them goodbye.

Sarah and Bill were smiling and speaking animatedly to each other as they left. They both thanked Fr. Sam for the session.

PASTORAL SKILLS FOR COUPLE CARE

Fr. Sam used the three sets of pastoral skills of the metanoia model—presence, proclamation, and guidance[1]—to help Sarah and Bill explore, understand, and act. He used the presence skills to help them explore their relationship and their reasons for wanting a church marriage; the proclamation skills to challenge Bill and Sarah's belief that they did not need much premarital care; and guidance skills to assist the couple in planning the tasks that lead to a wedding at St. Paul's.

Presence Skills

The presence skills, attending and responding, help pastors to empathize—to understand things from parishioners' (those receiving pastoral care) points of view. These skills also aid pastors in communicating their empathy and respect to parishioners. More important, attending and responding further parishioners' exploration of their issues. Because these skills both promote and express empathy and foster exploration, they are the key relationship-building skills.

Attending. In attending, pastors pay attention to parishioners by *positioning* themselves to communicate attentiveness, *observing* parishioners' nonverbal signals, and *listening* to both their words and their manner of speaking. Attending communicates interest and provides information, two foundations for the pastoral relationship.

Attending to couples involves noticing both each partner individually and the couple. That is, one must be attentive to the position, nonverbals, and words and manner of speaking of each partner, while also focusing on the way the partners position themselves in relationship to each other and communicate with each other verbally and nonverbally.

Positioning. In positioning, pastors situate their bodies to communicate interest. Gerard Egan in *The Skilled Helper* (1982, 60–61) lists five aspects of helpful positioning: (1) Face the [parishioners] *Squarely*, (2) adopt an *Open* position (uncrossed arms and legs), (3) *Lean* toward the [parishioner], (4) maintain good *Eye contact*, (5) try to be relatively *Relaxed*. He summarized these five—Squarely, Open, Lean, Eye contact, and Relaxed—in the acronym SOLER.

Because the meaning of eye contact, leaning forward, and squarely facing differ in different cultures, the degree to which these aspects are helpful varies. The SOLER position communicates interest to the dominant American culture, but aspects of it may not be comfortable for various subcultural groups or for particular individuals. Thus, pastors who minister to those outside of the dominant European-American subculture must develop ways of attending that are suitable for their parishioners.

When Fr. Sam sat facing Sarah and Bill leaning slightly forward with his hands loosely on his knees, he was in the SOLER position. The pastor prepared for the couple by placing two chairs fairly close together about six feet in front of the chair he would sit in so that he could see both of them at the same time, and maintain eye contact. When Sarah and Bill came in and sat down, Sarah pulled her chair slightly forward and sat leaning forward. Bill did not move his chair forward, so he was slightly behind her leaning back in his chair. He reaped another benefit of the SOLER position, in that it helps pastors to attend to the parishioners' nonverbals.

Observing. Observing involves being attentive to the messages parishioners communicate through their bodies. These messages are expressed through posture, facial expression, visual focus, movements, and involuntary responses such as the speed and depth of breathing, blushing, crying, and sighing. Observing generates very important data because nonverbal cues are the most common ways to communicate feelings, and nonverbal cues are usually more reliable than verbal expressions. Observing includes making provisional interpretations of the data.

One of the first nonverbals Fr. Sam observed was the couples' posture at the beginning of the session: Sarah pulled her chair forward and leaned forward and Bill left his chair back and leaned back. He interpreted this data to mean that Sarah was more interested in the session than Bill. During the session Fr. Sam noticed that Bill began leaning forward during the discussion of the questions and continued this way throughout the session; he read this as a sign of engagement. Fr. Sam also noticed how often Sarah and Bill looked at each other when issues came up, and understood that to mean that they consult each other; they do not function as singles.

Listening. Listening means noticing parishioners' words and manner of speaking. Spoken messages combine verbal content and nonverbal delivery. Listening involves heeding and making interpretations based on both types of data. Of the two, manner of speaking is often more revealing.

The first thing that Fr. Sam noticed about the couple's manner of speaking was that Sarah spoke first and most, with Bill's contributions serving as responses or additions. At the beginning, he didn't know whether to interpret this as a function of Bill's lack of engagement or to understand it as their normal pattern. When it persisted after Bill seemed more engaged (leaned forward), Fr. Sam decided that it was their pattern. Another manner of speaking that the pastor discerned was Bill's rapid speech around the issue of complementarity. Fr. Sam understood this as indicating that Bill had some issues about their differences that he was not expressing. The long pause, when asked about their reasons for a church wedding, was a third example of manner of speaking that Fr. Sam perceived. He presumed that this behavior meant that their reasons were not worked through very well. These and other manners of speaking provided valuable information about Bill and Sarah as a couple and as individuals.

The initial concerns illustrate how the combination of manner of speaking and content leads to interpretations. The position in which these questions are raised indicates that they are of great importance to those who ask them. Sarah's question about wedding date, and her volunteering of information about the wedding preparations, probably means that she is taking the lead in this arena and that it means a lot to her. Likewise, Bill's query about the cost of using the church implies that this is his responsibility and that the financial aspects of the wedding concern him very much. Thus the combination of manner of speaking and content provides rich material for hypotheses about Bill's and Sarah's issues and concerns.

The attending skills of positioning, observing, and listening provide the foundation for all other skills. These three skills generate the data to which the responding skills respond.

Responding. Paraphrases, probes, and summaries make up the responding skills. Paraphrases restate the core of a parishioner's statements in the pastor's own words. Probes ask for clarification. Summaries pull together the relevant data from observing, listening, paraphrasing, and probing into a succinct presentation of the parishioner's view of a situation.

Pastors use the responding skills to aid parishioners in exploring their issues. Paraphrases, probes, and summaries help parishioners in two important ways: (1) They let parishioners rehear what they are saying and thereby deepen their self-understanding; (2) they reflect to the parishioners how they are being understood, thus either helping them to understand themselves better or giving them an opportunity to correct the pastor's misconceptions.

The process of putting parishioners' feelings, experiences, actions, and thoughts in their own words helps pastors to understand parishioners better.

Responding skills are often used with couples to help them explore together. For instance, a pastor may paraphrase the core of both partners' statements as one. Fr. Sam did this when he observed, "You both feel good about the fact that you are very different." Similarly, summaries pull together the relevant data from observing, listening to, responding to, and probing both partners. Such was the case when Fr. Sam said, "You are saying that your both being different has been a help to each other and a positive thing, and you both feel very good about it." Probes are often used to involve the other partner in the conversation. Fr. Sam did this after Bill had talked about complementarity, when he asked Sarah, "How would you talk about it?"

It is important that paraphrases and summaries be nonjudgmental. Paraphrases and summaries should restate parishioners' understandings without either positive or negative input from pastors. Though frustrated by their resistance to premarital care, Fr. Sam said, "You wonder if six sessions are necessary because you know each other pretty well and the service seems simple." He did not say, "Even though this is very important for your future, you wonder if six sessions are necessary because you know each other pretty well and the service seems simple." If Fr. Sam had shared his own bias in this latter manner, he might have diverted Bill and Sarah from exploring their own issues and instead caused them to focus on his concerns about their future.

Probes should help parishioners to focus on their issues, not on the pastor's. Thus, questions should be open-ended so that people can respond to them on their terms and not the questioner's. That is why Fr. Sam asked Sarah an open-ended question—"How would you talk about it?"—instead of closed one such as, "Do you think being different is a good or a bad thing?" Similarly, probes are to be nonjudgmental; they are to clarify, not indict. Thus, Fr. Sam did not ask, "Do you really think that being so different is a good thing?" Judgmental and closed questions focus parishioners on the questioner's issues and divert them from their own exploration.

Summary of presence skills. The presence skills of attending (positioning, observing, and listening) and responding (paraphrasing, probing, and summarizing) build the foundation of pastoral conversations. They generate data and express the pastor's concern and understanding. The skills facilitate parishioners' exploration, drawing out and clarifying their feelings and thoughts so that they better understand their own perspectives. As skills designed to help persons explore their own issues, paraphrasing, probing, and summarizing must be nonjudgmental, and probes must be open-ended. Because opening sessions are primarily exploratory, Fr. Sam relied on the presence skills for most of the session.

Proclamation Skills

Proclamation skills differ from presence skills. While the presence skills focus on parishioners' exploration, the proclamation skills address parishioners' understanding. The presence skills keep pastors from inserting their agenda, while the proclamation skills direct the pastors' sharing of their concerns so that they best serve parishioners' understanding.

Proclamation skills both draw out the parishioners' understandings and challenge or support them. Thus, proclamation skills include assessing, challenging, and reviewing skills.

Assessing. The assessing skills, eliciting and hunching, help detect the beliefs that sustain parishioners' feelings and actions. *Eliciting* uses questions to draw out beliefs. *Hunching* expresses guesses about parishioners' beliefs, to help them make explicit their implied perspectives. Fr. Sam used eliciting when he followed up the couple's answers to the question about church marriage by asking, "What do you want this special blessing to do for your relationship?" This question drew out Bill's beliefs (1) about the importance of the good thoughts or prayers of the people at the wedding and (2) that blessing comes from public dedication. It also brought out Sarah's belief that "God's blessing makes the marriage holy and God will protect it because it is holy." And this question also disclosed that Bill was uncomfortable with Sarah's beliefs. These beliefs are important to know, as they are the reason the couple is choosing a church wedding. The pastor must challenge or build on these beliefs as he attempts to teach about marriage.

Challenging. The challenging skills (informing, sharing, confronting, and contending) endeavor to change unhelpful beliefs and support helpful ones. *Informing* is communicating needed information and correcting harmful misinformation. *Sharing* consists of offering a portion of the pastor's experience to parishioners. *Confronting* invites parishioners to examine the differences between their perceptions and the pastor's. *Contending* involves using reason and religious resources to dispute parishioners' unhelpful beliefs.

The proclamation skills require a base of exploration before they are used. That is why Fr. Sam paraphrased Sarah's and Bill's concerns about the six sessions, and why he waited for their affirmations that the paraphrase was accurate before he challenged them using proclamation skills.

Fr. Sam used sharing and informing in negotiating the contract. He used sharing when he said, "It's been my experience that couples have issues to work through no matter how long or how intensely they have know each other. I have worked with a lot of couples who have lived together one, two, or three years before preparing to get married, and they all found that they had issues to discuss." This is the skill of sharing because he used a portion of his experience to challenge the couple's unhelpful belief that they did not need to do much premarital work.

When Fr. Sam explained how the session would help them get the blessing they had said they wanted, he was using the skill of informing. He was communicating needed information about the connection of preparation to blessing to combat the harmful misinformation that the blessing came without preparation. Fr. Sam's use of informing was particularly skillful because he used the couples' stated desire for a blessing to challenge their belief that they did not need six sessions for marriage preparation. This demonstrates the importance of the couple's exploration and the pastor's assessment as a foundation for challenging.

Reviewing. There is one concluding proclamation skill, namely, reviewing. Reviewing involves inviting parishioners to summarize their understandings after they have been challenged.

Unlike presence skills, it is unlikely that pastors would use all of the proclamation skills in one conversation. Pastors choose the appropriate one or ones from the cluster. For example, Fr. Sam did not use the proclamation skills of hunching, confronting, contending, and reviewing during the opening session. Contending will be used later by Fr. Sam and Dr. Washington as they challenge the couples' beliefs with Scripture. Dr. Washington will use reviewing in teaching Scripture.

The proclamation skills of eliciting, hunching, informing, sharing, confronting, contending, and reviewing are means by which pastors aid parishioners in their understanding. They help, first, in assessing or drawing out the parishioners' beliefs, and then in challenging the unhelpful perspectives and supporting the helpful. These skills are based on the foundation of the parishioners' exploration.

Guidance Skills

After exploration and understanding, it is time to plan action. Pastors use guidance skills to help couples with action plans. These skills include setting goals, developing programs, and planning implementation. Goal setting involves establishing a concrete objective. Developing programs consists of creating activities to meet the objective, including choosing steps, scheduling, and creating reinforcements. Planning implementation includes reviewing, rehearsing, and revising the program, three sub-skills that prepare persons to carry out their program.

Setting goals and developing programs were all part of negotiating the contract in Fr. Sam's opening session with Sarah and Bill. Their goal was to have a wedding. The program that was developed was six sessions of premarital care. The steps of the program were the opening session, three meetings to discuss issues in their relationship, and two to work on planning the wedding in light of those issues. There would also be a wedding rehearsal. Working together, the pastor and couple scheduled the dates for the next five meetings and the rehearsal. The implied reinforcement was that Fr. Sam would not do the wedding if the couple did not complete the sessions.

Planning implementation (reviewing, rehearsing, and revising the program) will happen in connection with the wedding. The couple and pastor will review the service, revise it to fit their issues, and then rehearse it. Fr. Sam will use this skill in helping Sarah and Bill to adjust their prayer assignment.

The guidance skills of setting goals, developing programs, and planning implementation (and their sub-skills) provide a rich collection of tools from which pastors can choose. Action plans can be more or less elaborate depending on what is needed. The action plan for Sarah and Bill's wedding was elaborate, with six sessions and a rehearsal for steps, each prescheduled, with the reinforcement of the pastor's right to cancel the service. In addition some of the sessions were designated for reviewing, rehearsing, and revising. An action plan can be as simple as the agenda for a session, as when Fr. Sam negotiated the session agenda with Sarah and Bill.

The pastoral skills of presence, proclamation, and guidance are a pastor's tools for assisting couple growth and developing good pastoral relationships. These skills help couples to do the exploring, understanding, and acting that their premarital tasks require. Pastors who intend to communicate empathy and respect effectively must learn these skills.

Structuring Tactics

Structuring involves shaping a session so that couples can feel safe to explore, understand, and act. Fr. Sam used two structuring tactics in the opening session: engaging both partners, and regulating the depth of inquiry. These tactics create a safe space for the couple and thus encourage them to engage their issues.

Engaging both partners. Engaging both partners means helping both to participate actively in the session. The need for structuring conversations so that both partners are engaged is one of the major differences between interviews with individuals and those with couples and families. With individuals there is no competition for "air time," but with couples and families, concern about getting one's point of view heard is a major issue. When each partner knows that his or her contribution will be heard and respected, he or she will be more relaxed and able to listen to both the pastor and the other partner.

There are many techniques for engaging both partners. Involving the least engaged partner in the conversation by asking questions of them is one method of engaging both partners. Fr. Sam did this when he offered Bill equal time for an initial question, after handling Sarah's initial question about the wedding date and then setting the agenda. Another way of engaging both partners is to ensure that both offer their responses to an important issue. For example, Fr. Sam asked Bill, "How would you tell the story of how the two of you decided to get married?" after Sarah had responded to that same question.

Engaging both partners lets each partner know that she or he will have a chance to be heard and to have her or his contribution respected. This tactic constitutes one important way of structuring the session to make couples feel safe.

Regulating the depth of inquiry. Regulating the depth of inquiry consists of consciously governing the level of responses made to the couple. Persons' comfort with revealing themselves correlates with their comfort in relating to the pastor. Asking persons to reveal themselves too deeply early in the relationship often results in poor responses, withdrawal, or a termination of the relationship. Conversely, helping persons to share on a less profound level builds the relationship. Therefore, it is important to begin the course of sessions with more surface sharing, using the earlier conversations to build the relationship for deeper probes later.

Fr. Sam regulated the depth of his inquiry several times during the opening session. For instance, after summarizing the couples' responses about their differences, Fr. Sam wanted to pursue their responses more. But remembering that the couple was just getting to know him, he held back. Though Fr. Sam pushed deeper in the discussion of why they wanted a church wedding by drawing out their understandings of blessing, he held back by not challenging their beliefs.

There are several factors to be considered in regulating the depth of inquiry: (a) the position of the session in the course of sessions, (b) one's place in a particular session, and (c) the responses of the couple. Pastors generally regulate the depth of their inquiry by starting with the more superficial levels in the opening sessions and moving to deeper levels in later sessions. Likewise, it is usually appropriate to begin a conversation at one level and then allow the inquiry to get more profound as it progresses. As an example, Fr. Sam went deeper with the discussion on church weddings than in the previous discussion. After due consideration of factors (a) and (b), it is important to respond appropriately whenever couples signal their willingness to go deeper through initiating sharing on a more profound level.

Regulating the depth of inquiry ensures that the scope of the discussion does not exceed couples' willingness to engage. The tactic of regulating the depth of inquiry constitutes a second way of structuring conversations to make couples feel secure.

Learning the Skills

The best way to learn the pastoral skills and structuring tactics is through practicing them in a group. Practice groups should contain three or four people: one to play the pastor role, two to play the couple, and a fourth, if available, to be the observer. Each person plays each role during a practice session. When the group has only three people, a videotape or audiotape can be used as the observer.

A single role-play proceeds in this manner. The pastor and couple act out a situation other than their own, with the couple and the observer paying special attention to the pastor's skill strengths and growth areas. After the role-play, the couple, then the pastor, debriefs feelings or issues arising from their interaction. If available, the observer moderates the debriefing. When the group completes debriefing, first the couple and then the observer give specific feedback to the pastor on his or her skills. The pastor receives this feedback and speaks only to ask questions of clarification.

The learning in practice groups can be made even more effective by (1) taping the sessions and replaying them during the feedback so that all can see and/or hear exactly what happened, instead of relying only on their different memories, and (2) having a counselor trained in helping skills supervise the group.

In addition to the examples and definitions of the pastoral skills in this chapter, there are more examples and exercises for learning these skills in *The Skilled Pastor* (Taylor 1991).

Conclusion

The pastoral skills and structuring tactics provide two tools that pastors need to be helpful. The presence skills of attending and responding help couples explore their issues. The proclamation skills of assessing, challenging, and reviewing package pastors' insights in ways that help couples better to understand their issues. The guidance skills of goal setting, developing programs, and planning implementation help couples plan their action effectively. Finally, structuring tactics such as engaging both partners, and regulating the depth of inquiry, shape conversations in ways that make couples feel safe. The pastoral skills and the structuring tactics enhance pastoral relationships and couple growth.

In addition to pastoral skills and structuring tactics, two other tools, the design of the sessions and the methods of raising premarital issues, contribute to pastoral helpfulness. While the conversation at the beginning of this chapter illustrates these tools, Chapter 3 contains a full discussion of them.

3

SESSION COMPONENTS
AND TOPICS

How should sessions be put together? Should opening sessions be constructed differently from subsequent sessions? What subjects need to be dealt with in the opening session and in subsequent sessions? How are these topics introduced? This chapter addresses each of these questions. First, summaries of an opening and a subsequent marriage-preparation conversation led by Dr. Washington illustrate the components of the sessions. This is followed by a discussion of the components. Then the chapter introduces the important topics to be covered in premarital guidance. A discussion of the types of programs for introducing these topics completes this chapter.

The discussion of the components comes first because a good framework provides a necessary condition for learning and couple counseling. A regularly used framework makes couples feel safe, helps them to participate, and assures them that they will be heard.

A clear agreement on time requirements constitutes a major part of the session's framework. I suggest 50-minute-long individual sessions, 90-minute-long couple sessions, and 150-minute-long group sessions.

THE OPENING SESSIONS

In the opening session, the pastor should strive to involve the couple in the church's premarital guidance program by establishing a pastoral relationship and presenting the church's program in a way that relates the couple's issues to the pastoral resources.

Establishing a Relationship

The pastoral relationship constitutes the primary vehicle for couple involvement in the opening session. A pastoral relationship develops as the pastor gets to know the couple as the couple, and the couple gets to know the pastor as premarital caregiver.

Even if pastors know one or both partners well as individuals, they have to start at the beginning with the partners as a couple. Today's younger adults and educated adults of all ages often do not automatically grant pastors authority. Rather, they test pastors by judging the amount of genuineness, acceptance, and respect they communicate. Therefore pastors need to develop the relationship with couples before they challenge them very much. This means that rather than plunging right in during the opening session, pastors should emphasize the presence skills (Chap. 2) of attending and responding. Pastors should wait until later sessions to work through issues in depth.

To deepen the relationship between the couple's issues and tasks and religious resources defines the goal of subsequent sessions. The early subsequent sessions focus on exploring and expanding the couple's understanding of their needs. In these early sessions, the pastor is the primary religious resource. In the later sessions, the couple set their issues and insights in the context of such religious resources as Scripture and the wedding rite. This chapter focuses on the components and topics of the early sessions. Chapters 5 and 6 discuss the later sessions with Scripture and the wedding rite.

In addition to illustrating the basic ingredients of marriage-preparation sessions, the following summaries of an opening session with Wilma and Rich, and Wilma's individual session with Dr. Washington, show some of this couple's issues and Dr. Washington's strategies for dealing with their preparation for remarriage.

Opening Session of Dr. Washington, Wilma, and Rich

Initial concerns. Rich began the session by asking if the recentness of his divorce was a problem for Dr. Washington. The pastor responded that the previous marriage is always an issue when preparing for a new marriage; thus they needed to set aside a time to discuss it. Rich tried to lure Dr. Washington into an immediate discussion of this matter, but the pastor was firm about needing to meet with Rich alone. Wilma's initial concern was about having a Christian marriage. She said that they both wanted to do it right this time.

Setting agenda. Dr. Washington then proposed a simple agenda: (a) She would ask them a few questions to get to know them better; (b) she would explain the GMZ premarital program; (c) if they agreed to the program, they would fill out a premarital inventory; and (d) they would give her a proposed wedding date, wedding party names, addresses, and other basic information about themselves and the wedding. She then asked if they had anything to add to the agenda. When they said no, she asked if they agreed to it, and they did.

Exploring understanding. After obtaining their consent to the agenda, Dr. Washington proceeded by asking them to tell her about their journey to marriage. They told her that they had met about eighteen months ago through a mutual friend, about six months after Rich and his previous wife, Helen, had separated. The past year was difficult for them because of the strain on Rich of a difficult divorce from Helen and the difficulties that Wilma had with her former husband, Henry, and their two girls. As Dr. Washington listened to the issues they were struggling with, she understood why Wilma and Rich did not have the usual silly engaged-couple grins on their faces.

Because the couple had initiated the discussion of Christian marriage, the pastor asked what a Christian marriage meant to them. They agreed that it was one built on biblical guidelines, church participation, and God's love.

Negotiating contracts. Because they came looking for help, they were ready for a serious preparation. Dr. Washington contracted with them for participation in a six-week Sunday morning class for couples that she would teach called "Growing Together," plus one couple session on the biblical meaning of marriage and one couple session on planning the wedding ritual, and the wedding rehearsal. Because they were preparing for remarriage, she contracted with them for three special sessions: two individual sessions, one for each to discuss what he or she had learned from their previous marriage, and one couple session to share their learnings. She then suggested that they attend a relationship skills (communication and conflict resolution) workshop during their first year of marriage. Wilma and Rich accepted this suggestion as part of their program. After affirming this contract, they spent thirty minutes filling out the premarital inventory.

Getting information. They concluded the session by establishing the basic information about their individual addresses, phone numbers, previous spouses, dates of divorce, children, proposed wedding date, wedding party, and other such details.

Summary of the Individual Conversation with Wilma

Background. Wilma and Dr. Washington met two weeks after the opening session for a session on what Wilma learned from her first marriage. Dr. Washington had set up this session to see how conscious Wilma was of her contributions to the problems of the previous marriage. The computer report on the inventory indicated that Wilma lacked assertiveness,[2] which is a destructive factor in couple communication.

Initial concerns. Wilma's initial concern was whether this meeting was an investigation into who caused the divorce. After Dr. Washington assured her that the purpose was to discuss the insights and concerns that she brought from the previous marriage, Wilma was ready to discuss the one agenda item.

Reviewing preparation. Dr. Washington then asked Wilma what she had thought about during the past two weeks in considering the lessons from her previous marriage. Wilma replied that she thought a lot about how difficult it was for Henry to accept her as a peer. She related that she had married him when she was very young and willing to go along with his "bossiness." But when she gained more self-confidence through her career, it became more difficult to acquiesce to Henry, and he wouldn't accept a change to a more equal relationship. So they just argued and argued and got nowhere. Then she would try to keep silent and hold on for the children's sake, but she could only do that so long. So Wilma sought advice from some of the church mothers and from the pastor. They all had urged her to follow the Bible's teaching and submit; she tried and tried but she just couldn't continue being that way. When she had finally had enough, she got a divorce. She concluded that she had learned that she needed a relationship in which she was considered an equal.

Expanding understanding. When Dr. Washington pressed her on how she contributed to this problem, Wilma was not clear at first. After considerable help from the pastor, Wilma began to see that her initial acquiescence, and her vacillation between submitting and claiming her equality, had been some part of the problem. Wilma tried to move the subject to her present problems with dealing with her ex-husband and the children. Dr. Washington resisted this attempt, so that she could help Wilma see more clearly how her own lack of assertiveness contributed to her marital problems.

Negotiating contracts. With the time for the session nearing an end, Dr. Washington decided to negotiate two contracts with Wilma. The first contract concerned the issues that Wilma would bring from this individual session to the joint session. After some discussion Wilma decided to bring her concern about being treated as an equal and her need for Rich's support in being more assertive. The second agreement that Dr. Washington sought involved Wilma committing to do further work in assertiveness training, such as attending one of GMZ's workshops on this issue. After a brief discussion, Wilma agreed to seek help in this area. The session ended with Wilma commenting that this was a very tough but helpful session. She then thanked the pastor and left.

SESSION COMPONENTS

Marriage-preparation sessions have six components: handling initial concerns, reviewing preparation, setting the agenda, exploring and expanding understandings, negotiating contracts, and getting information.

Handling Initial Concerns

Handling the initial concerns consists of introductions and respectful responses to the opening questions or first issues raised by the couple.

This first component of the session provides an opportunity for the pastor to break the ice by engaging the couple at the point of their most intense interest. This ice breaking is crucial in the opening session and remains important in each subsequent session. By responding to the initial concerns as they are raised, the pastor models respect by showing regard for what interests the couple. Conversely, not responding to initial concerns indicates too much focus on the pastor's own agenda.

Responding to initial concerns does not mean discussing them fully at that time. When it would not be helpful to deal with the issue at that time, then the pastor should state when and how she or he will deal with it. For example, in Dr. Washington's opening session with Wilma and Rich, Rich's initial concern was about whether Dr. Washington had a problem with the recentness of his divorce. After responding that the previous marriage is always an issue when preparing for a new marriage, Dr. Washington refused to be led into the discussion at that time because this issue would be best discussed in an individual session.

The couple's initial concerns give valuable information. For instance, Rich's concern about Dr. Washington's feelings about his recent divorce indicated the importance of this issue for him. Likewise, Wilma's concern for a Christian marriage revealed her major interest.

Reviewing Preparation

Reviewing preparation involves a discussion of the couples' progress on their assignment. This review includes raising the following questions about missed homework: What got in the way of it? When will this session be rescheduled, if it is dependent on the homework?

Engaged couples prepare for marriage and the pastor helps them, not vice versa. Thus, the homework is important. When a couple does their homework, they are ready to raise their issues and to ask their questions. This allows the pastor to respond directly to their issues and perceptions, instead of giving a generalized lecture on the subject. Thus, reviewing preparation shows that the pastor takes the couple's contribution seriously, and the review invites the couple to take it seriously also.

Setting the Agenda

Setting the agenda, the third component, involves working with the couple to determine which topics are to be covered in a session. Their participation in creating and consenting to the agenda involves them in the session. For example, during the opening session above, Dr. Washington shared her agenda and explained it. Then she asked for Wilma and Rich's input and consent. Setting the agenda continues to be important in subsequent sessions because it gives the comfort of framework to couple conversations.

Exploring and Expanding Understandings

The fourth component of a marriage-preparation session consists of exploring and expanding the couple's understandings—in other words, discussing an issue or issues at some depth to uncover the couple's views. Expanding understandings means that the pastor challenges the uncovered understandings.

Opening sessions focus primarily on exploring understandings, but subsequent sessions explore and expand the couple's understandings. For example, Dr. Washington used two probes—"Tell me about your journey to marriage" and "What does a Christian marriage mean to you?"—to explore the couple's understandings in an opening session. By contrast, after Dr. Washington helped Wilma explore what she had learned from the divorce in a subsequent session, the pastor challenged her to think about her contribution to the problems in that marriage.

One important technique for expanding understandings involves limiting the conversation to a few issues and discussing them deeply. This technique is important because there is neither the time nor the possibility of covering everything. Treating one issue produces lessons that have a profound effect on the whole relationship. Thus, Wilma and Dr. Washington focused on what Wilma learned from her divorce, even though Wilma tried to change the subject to another important area.

A second effective technique for expanding understandings consists of exploring their understandings first, then challenging any unhelpful beliefs or significant omissions using proclamation skills (Chap. 2). This happened in Dr. Washington's session with Wilma. Dr. Washington first asked Wilma what lessons she had learned from her marriage to Henry. Upon hearing that her lesson applied to the type of husband she needed but did not include Wilma's own contribution to the problem, Dr. Washington challenged Wilma to identify her own part in maintaining the bad situation.

Negotiating Contracts

The fifth important component, negotiating the contract, consists of agreeing on the next steps to take and who will do what. Agreeing on the nature of the premarital guidance program constitutes the major negotiation in an opening session. In the example of Dr. Washington, Wilma, and Rich, the program was a class, five couple sessions, a wedding rehearsal, and a communication workshop during their first year of marriage.

Negotiating contracts in subsequent sessions often involves establishing the preparation the pastor and couple will make for the next session. For example, during Wilma's individual session, she and Dr. Washington each negotiated what issues they would bring to their joint session and what further work Wilma would do on the issue of assertiveness.

Getting Information

Getting information, a sixth component usually found in opening sessions, involves recording necessary facts about the couple. This basic information puts the conversation in context by beginning to answer the key factual questions about the couple: Do they live together, are they church members, have they been married before? It also lets the pastor know more about the couple's relationship by showing how they answer questions (for example, who answers which questions and how). Finally, such information as home and e-mail addresses, and telephone, pager, and fax numbers helps the pastor contact the couple in case a session has to be rescheduled, information has to be obtained from them, or material has to be sent to them.

This component comes last because the necessity for this information depends on the couple's acceptance of the premarital program.

Summary of Components Section

The frameworks of opening sessions and subsequent sessions usually share four components: initial concerns, setting the agenda, exploring and expanding understandings, and negotiating contracts. Getting information is the fifth and final component in the opening session, whereas reviewing preparation, which comes after initial concerns, completes the set of five components in subsequent sessions.

TOPICS

A stable group of topics appears in a variety of writings on premarital guidance (Clinebell 1975; Dyer and Dyer 1990; Grenz and Glover 1996; Hunt and Hunt 1982; Midgley and Midgley 1992; Mittman 1980; Olson 1996; Velander 1993). Each structured interview, inventory, workbook, or course noted above contains many or most of the following topics:

1. Communication. Does each partner feel heard by the other? Do they feel comfortable sharing feelings with each other? Does each partner understand the feelings and reasons for these feelings that the other states?

2. Conflict resolution. Does the couple have the ability to solve problems and come to mutually agreed-upon solutions, without destructive side effects?

3. Role relationship. Does the couple have a mutually agreed-upon understanding of their marital roles, whether companionship or traditional?

4. Sexuality. Does each partner understand the other's sexual needs and desires? Are both partners comfortable with their present sexual relationship?

5. Values, religion, spirituality. Does each partner understand and support the other partner's core values, religious understandings, and spiritual practice? What are their plans for nurturing individual and couple values, as well as religious or spiritual expression?

6. Children. Do both partners want to have children? If so, how many? How will they be guided, and by whom? How will children from previous relationships be handled?

7. Family of origin and friends. What level of approval or disapproval of the couple's relationship do each partner's family of origin (parents, siblings, aunts, uncles, cousins, and grandparents) and friends have? How does each partner feel about his or her own family of origin? What traits of their family of origin does each partner want to or not want to carry into their marriage?

8. Relaxation, leisure, interests. What are the activities each partner does for relaxation and a change of pace? What shared activities do they have? Which activities do each want to continue alone?

9. Personality/relating style. Does either partner act in ways that trouble or embarrass the other? What characteristics does each partner treasure in the other?

10. Finances. What resources does each partner bring to the marriage? How are the resources to be used? Have they agreed on a budget?

11. Marriage expectations. What expectations does each partner have about marriage? How realistic or unrealistic are these expectations?

The structured interviews, inventories, workbooks, and courses that contain these topics recommend that couples preparing for marriage take account of most of these areas in their process of preparation. Common sense indicates the importance of these topics for the longevity and happiness of marriages because these are the areas about which couples struggle, fight, and divorce. Conversely, many couples credit their happiness and continuance as couples to unity in some combination of these areas. Research (Flowers 1986, Larsen 1989, Olson 1993) indicates that positive couple agreement on many of these topics during the premarital period correlates strongly with marital happiness. Conversely, the lack of positive agreement correlates strongly with unhappiness, separation, and divorce.

Another important approach is skills training in communication and conflict resolution. Research pioneered by Gottman (1979, 1989) and Markman et al. (1988, 1993) indicates that the absence of these skills predicts failure in marriage relationships in over 80 percent of couples. John Gottman's *Why Marriages Succeed or Fail* (1994) and Markman, Stanley, and Blumberg's *Fighting for Your Marriage* (1994) present conflict-resolution skills training programs based on their groundbreaking research.

On the other hand, several significant writers on premarital guidance, such as Herbert Anderson (Anderson and Fite 1993: Anderson and Mitchell 1993), Edwin Friedman (1985, 1989), and Stahmann and Hiebert (1987) take an entirely different approach, focusing most sessions on one topic: the couple's families of origin. Their rationale includes the following points: (1) The wedding and marriage are family transitional events; therefore, they are best prepared for by an understanding of the families involved. (2) Each partner's family of origin is his or her primary teacher about marriage; therefore, making what they have learned conscious to the one partner and available to the other partner prepares them for marriage. (3) The ability to disengage from one's family of origin constitutes the key factor in the ability to engage with one's partner. Reflecting on the family of origin helps partners both to disengage and to identify those family relationships that need more work. (4) Since marriage is a "wedding of stories" (Anderson and Foley 1990), knowing and sharing the family stories is foundational. (5) Couples preparing for marriage are much less defensive about and more open to learning about their families of origin than they are about their own issues.

Despite these powerful arguments for the family of origin as the main focus of premarital guidance, I recommend the multiple-topics and skills-training approaches because they are supported by considerable scientific research. The family-of-origin approach has a wealth of clinical impressions behind it but lacks a comparable support of rigorous studies. Because of the importance of the family of origin, the best marriage-preparation programs combine the multiple-topics and skills-training approaches with a special emphasis on the family of origin.

INTRODUCING THE TOPICS

The topics are usually addressed by one or more of four methods: structured interviews, inventories, workbooks, and courses. The following discussion introduces and evaluates each of these methods. Appendix A contains a detailed discussion of selected examples of these methods.

(1) Structured interviews. Structured interviews are sessions in which the pastor follows a planned list of questions and topics. This type of interview has several advantages over a nonstructured interview. First, it gives the pastor a clear direction for the course of care. Second, it provides a definite framework for care. Third, it assures that the important topics will be raised.

The opening session of Fr. Sam with Sarah and Bill was a structured interview. Each of the five components generated a portion of the opening session's content. The necessary introductions and the couple's initial concerns provided the early content. Setting the agenda organized the content of the session. Introductory questions to the couple—such as "How did you decide to get married?" and "Why do you want to get married in a church?" elicited the content for the exploring understandings component. The discussion of a premarital program and working toward an agreed program provided the content for the negotiation component. When the program was agreed upon, then the final content was the basic information about the couple.

There are several weaknesses to structured interviews when they are used for subsequent sessions without other resources. First, the resultant lack of homework underemphasizes the couple's participation and overemphasizes the pastor's role. Second, the absence of written instruction on the topics leaves the couple with no more than the partners can remember during this stressful time. Third, precious session time is consumed in getting the information on the partner's views, which could be obtained by inventories. Because of these weaknesses, I do not recommend the use of structured interviews, without other resources, for marriage preparation.

(2) Workbooks. Workbooks provide information and exercises for the couple to use without the presence of a third person. One strength is that they provide solid information on most of the topics. Another is their emphasis on the importance of the couples' participation in their marriage preparation. Finally, they suggest exercises and questions that help the couple to learn experientially.

The workbook method, when used alone, has several weaknesses. First, the absence of a third person means that there is no one to observe the couple's communication and conflict resolution. Second, this method lacks the objective party to help couples discuss difficult issues more comfortably and insightfully. Third, workbooks work best with the minority of people who learn primarily through reading. Finally, they assume that the quality of information, not the conflict-resolution skills and the positive couple agreement, provides the best basis for successful marriage, whereas the research (Gottmann 197; Gottman and Krokoff 1989; Markman et al. 1988, 1993) indicates that the depth of communication and positive couple agreement correlate strongly with happy marriages. Because of these weaknesses of the workbook method when used by itself, I do not recommend it for premarital guidance. Workbooks, however, can be used well with inventories or as part of a course.

(3) Inventories. Premarital inventories are questionnaires that focus on the partners' knowledge of and opinions about many of the topics listed above. They differ from personality tests in that premarital inventories measure the presence or absence of positive couple agreement on the topics, whereas personality tests focus on the individuals' feelings and individual personality issues.

Inventories reap more strategic information in a shorter time than interviews. Inventories help couples in several ways: (a) They challenge them to explore areas of their relationship that they usually have not thought much about; (b) they teach the couple the important issues for marriage by the questions they ask; (c) they provoke discussion between the partners about these relevant issues. In addition, inventories identify serious differences between the partners, a factor that has been shown to be correlated with unhappiness in marriage or divorce. The taking of premarital inventories, even without feedback sessions, has been shown to have a positive effect on marital satisfaction (Druckman et al. 1979).

The major weakness of inventories with feedback sessions is the relative lack of information conveyed on the topics. When feedback is given in individual sessions, the process suffers from the absence of a learning community. Premarital inventories are far superior to structured interviews and workbooks, however; research indicates that their use positively correlates with marital happiness. Therefore, I recommend the use of these inventories, preferably with feedback sessions, for use in marriage preparation. This is the type of program that Fr. Sam worked out with Sarah and Bill.

(4) Courses. Courses combine workbooks, leaders, and group interaction into a powerful premarital guidance program. They have the workbook strengths of topic coverage and couple participation, along with the structured interview strength of an active pastor and orderly issue coverage. Courses have the added strengths of a learning community: (a) the empowerment of seeing others in the same situation, (b) the aid of hearing others ask questions that one has oneself but has either not formulated or not asked, (c) opportunities for seeing good communication and conflict-resolution skills modeled, and (d) the chance to get feedback on one's practice of relationship skills.

Courses lack the intense pastor-to-couple relationship that individual feedback sessions provide, but the strengths of the learning community more than make up for this weakness for the couple, if not for some pastors. Used alone they lack the strengths of premarital inventories. Because of their many strengths, I recommend courses as the best of the four methods of marriage preparation. A combination of a course plus inventory, plus individual sessions, and a relationship-skills workshop provides a better marriage preparation. That is the type of program that Dr. Washington worked out with Wilma and Rich.

There are eleven topics frequently mentioned in the literature on premarital guidance: communication, conflict resolution, role relationship, sexuality, values or religion or spirituality, children, family of origin and friends, relaxation or leisure or interests, personality/relating style, finances, and marriage expectations.

Courses provide the best way to introduce the topics and teach relationship skills. Premarital inventory programs rank second. I do not recommend workbooks and structured interviews, used alone, for marriage preparation, because these methods do not measure couple agreement or teach relationship skills effectively. Combinations of courses or premarital inventories with workbooks provide the strongest ways to raise and explore the topics. The best programs put a special emphasis on the family of origin, because this topic relates to the partners' ability to engage with each other.

CONCLUSION

Dr. Washington organized Wilma and Rich's opening session with a framework of five components: handling initial concerns, agenda setting, exploring understandings, negotiating contracts, and getting information. These components provide a framework for setting up a pastoral relationship and presenting a marriage-preparation program. All of these components, except getting information, were carried over to subsequent sessions, assuring that the couple would have the advantage of a familiar yet comprehensive framework for their sessions. The content of the first session was mostly exploratory, as befits the beginning of a relationship. All eleven common topics were introduced in the opening session, however, through taking the Prepare Inventory. These topics would be further explored in the three feedback sessions for which they had contracted. During these feedback sessions, the couple's understandings of some of these topics, especially the family of origin, would be expanded.

This chapter on components and topics concludes the focus of the first part of premarital guidance: the discussion of methods for identifying and exploring the couples' issues. The next chapter provides a transition to the chapters that present methods for bringing these issues together with such religious resources as Scripture and the wedding service in the second part of premarital guidance.

4

COMMON
COUPLE TASKS

This chapter argues that the religious nature of the marriage journey links the couple's issues and the religious resources. It introduces the three fundamental tasks of the journey into marriage—getting a blessing, leaving, and cleaving—and the religious foundations of each. Scriptures, some of which are those often recommended for weddings, are used to show the relationship between pastoral resources and the common tasks.

The religious dimensions of these common tasks provide the link between couples' issues and the pastoral resources. Because the basic tasks in getting married are religious, the pastoral resources are uniquely appropriate to deal with these concerns. Thus, premarital guidance involves bringing together couples' issues and tasks with pastoral resources for religious marriage preparation.

Chapters 2 and 3 have focused on the skills and methods of bringing couples' issues to light. Chapters 5 and 6 focus on the skills and methods of relating the pastoral resources to couples' issues. Chapter 4 provides the transition between the issues-raising and the resource-relating stages of premarital guidance.

Each couple brings their own unique issues to premarital guidance. Three fundamental tasks, however, undergird most premarital issues: getting a blessing, leaving, and cleaving. Engaged couples want their relationship blessed by the church, the state, their family and friends; this is the reason for the wedding. In order to get this blessing through marriage, partners need to revise their old relationships in order to build a new marital relationship. The Bible calls the revising of old relationships "to leave" and the building of the marital relationship "to cleave (cling to, join with)" (Gen. 2:24; Matt. 19:5; Mark 10:7 KJV).

Most cultures consider getting the blessing, leaving, and cleaving to be religious tasks (Martos 1993, 32), because at their foundations they are profound experiences of union, powerfully felt invitations to leave the old and walk by faith, and exciting visions of new life that will be found in unfamiliar and foreboding places. These foundational experiences share with religious experiences the power to reorient lives and the sense of being unmerited gifts. Blessing, leaving, and cleaving are also religious in the sense that they involve couples' perspectives on life. The ways in which the partners understand these tasks reflect their world-views or theologies.

Christian theologians think of the religious nature of blessing, leaving, and cleaving in several ways, of which one is a natural-theology way and another a revealed-theology way. Natural theology holds these human tasks to be sacramental, God expressing Godself through natural human experiences. Revealed theology understands these profound human experiences to be analogous to the way God acts, instructive parables of God's grace. Either way the tasks of getting a blessing, leaving, and cleaving have profound religious meaning.

GETTING A BLESSING

The central task is getting a blessing. The word *blessing* has many different meanings woven together in it. It means dedication, for to bless something is to set it apart. Another meaning is to sanctify, to make holy. A related meaning is to protect; those things that are made holy are understood as protected by God. To bless is to give thanks for, as in the blessing before a meal. Bless also means to give approval, as when we say, "The parents gave the marriage their blessing." The couple comes to the Church or pastor to receive a blessing for their relationship.

The Bonding Process

Couples who come to the pastor to discuss a wedding are seeking a blessing of the marriage that, in a sense, has already happened to them. There is a four-step bonding or marrying process (Stahmann and Hiebert 1987, 132). The first step happens when each partner says to him- or herself "This person is for me." Second, each person begins to indicate to the other that he or she is held in special regard by telling the other, both verbally and nonverbally, "You are for me." In the third step, couples announce to others what has already happened to them individually and as a couple (engagement, plans to marry, living together). By this time they are usually psychologically married. Thus, when most couples come to the pastor they have already considered marriage and begun it; they just want to have a wedding so they can get their marriage blessed. The wedding is the fourth and most public step in the bonding process.

A Profound Experience

This process of psychological marriage is a profound experience. The partners have experienced union with each other. They feel complete, known, loved, appreciated, happy, full, excited, warm, and whole. They experience themselves as growing and flowering. Bonded couples consider their relationship as a precious gift given to them, a present from God (or the universe, or fate, or life). Thus gifted, they relate more kindly toward others and more hopefully toward the future.

This experience carries with it a sense of urgency. Now that the partners have found each other, they passionately want to be with each other right now and for eternity. As Bill said when he proposed, "Will you marry me? I can't live without you!" And lest one think these feelings are simply ideas or vague notions, be reminded that there are tremendous physical changes going on during this period. Their bodies are pumping endorphins and other special hormones. These secretions, which manifest themselves in the stereotypical "silly grin" and sense of well-being, are driving the couple toward union.

Despite all their fears and any external roadblocks, the couple is being pushed by powerful internal forces to get their marriage recognized and finalized. Thus it is very difficult for pastors or anyone else to change or stop this movement. In many cases, such attempts to intervene will be unsuccessful.

The Choice of Mates

If it is so difficult to intervene, then how accurate is their choice of mates? It is usually very accurate in terms of psychological needs; people tend to choose exactly the mate that they need *at that point in time* (Stahmann and Hiebert 1987, 18). People choose partners with the complementary psychological characteristics with which they need to struggle in order to grow. According to Harville Hendrix (1988, 8), people choose the mate who has a particular set of positive and negative personality traits that correspond with the predominant character traits of the people who raised them.

Why are they searching for a person with their caretakers' negative personality traits? According to Hendrix (1988, 45–46), they choose someone with opposite traits from themselves and more like their parents (or parental figures) in order to heal old wounds and grow in new areas. So the quiet, reserved Bill chooses the outgoing Sarah, who is as involved with people outside the family as his mother. He does this even though he experienced his mother's personality as intrusive as a child, and he felt abandoned by her because she was always leaving him to talk on the phone or attend a church meeting.

Complementarity Between Partners

When persons find a partner who represents their opposite side, their lives are transformed. The successful completion of this primal search fills them with a sense of self-esteem. The experience of someone like their parents listening to them in ways their parents did not makes them feel accepted. These feelings of self-esteem and acceptance are so powerful that they deaden the partners' sensitivity to the negatives of choosing a person who represents their unresolved issues. Instead they rejoice in the complementarity. Bill likes Sarah because she is the life of the party; she draws him out because he tends to be shy. Sarah likes Bill because he is so smart and self-sufficient that it is fun to learn from him.

Couples preparing for marriage feel only a little of the pain of complementarity. It bothers Bill a bit that Sarah wants to go out so much. He is heartened, however, by the fact that she has stayed in with him a lot the past seven months, and she seemed to enjoy learning the things he was teaching her. Thus he believes that she is becoming more mature and will be less driven to be out all the time after they are married. Likewise, Sarah expects that Bill will become more sociable after they get married because he has become so much more sociable since they started dating. She also thinks he sometimes gets a little long-winded and tedious when he explains things to her, but he seems to enjoy it and it doesn't bother her that much.

Yet part of the blessing they seek has to do with blessing their ambivalence about their complementarity. For example, Bill is excited about how much Sarah helps him to participate in parties, and he is a bit concerned about how much she wants to go out. Perhaps it was this ambivalence that caused Bill to talk more rapidly in the opening session when he said, "But we complement each other. I am helping her to think things out better and she is helping me to get out more." What he wants blessed is both his excitement about growth and his concern about a possible strain in the relationship. Thus, what both he and Sarah need is for Fr. Sam to help them celebrate their excitement and acknowledge their concern.

Though the possession of these complementary attributes has a lot to do with bonding, it has little to do with the capacity to sustain a relationship. In fact, they put peculiar strains on an ongoing relationship. Complementarity requires that partners deal with old, painful, and unresolved issues from their childhood. It also makes it necessary for couples to develop ways of being that honor and include opposite styles and points of view. Couples need three qualities to maintain a relationship against complementarity's destructive stresses: (1) the emotional freedom to disengage or leave their family of origin (and previous partners) in order to cleave to the new partner, (2) good communication and conflict-resolution skills, and (3) a foundation of shared values.

The Religious Dimension of Bonding

The experience of choosing a mate and bonding with that person can be described as a profoundly religious experience. As has been described above, the choosing and bonding process is intense. It is an experience of the union of parts long separated, the achieving of a wholeness long desired. The partners perceive that they have found that part of themselves that was lost in the mists before time. It is an experience of receiving the other as a gift from God.

The couple has had the type of experience that is so powerful, it is best described by the metaphors in the creation stories of the Bible. Genesis 1:27 tells us that both male and female were made in the image of God. This concept helps us to talk about each partner experiencing with the other that wholeness which signals the completion of God's image for them. Similarly, Genesis 2:21-23 depicts humans as being created in unity and then split into male and female. That picture leads to a description of the couple as having found in each other the other half of themselves. Those two biblical stories assert that the union of a man and a woman is blessed by God at the beginning of the world. Couples seek a wedding so that they can celebrate and maintain that blessing.

In addition to the sense of completeness, bonding provides an experience of growth and transformation. The partners' self-esteem grows and they exhibit a new appreciation of others and life itself. This change in perception and behavior parallels the Spirit's gift of love to the Christian community described in the First Letter to the Corinthians: "Love is patient; love is kind; love is not envious or boastful or arrogant or rude. It does not insist on its own way; it is not irritable or resentful; . . . It bears all things, believes all things, hopes all things, endures all things" (1 Cor. 13:4-5, 7).

Because the partners know that their relationship has made each of them more like this description, they want to bless their relationship by celebrating this gift that has been given to them. In addition, they want this growth and change to go on forever; they want their love to be as permanent as the one described here: "Love never ends" (1 Cor. 13: 8a). Thus they want their relationship blessed, both to secure their experience of transformation and to ensure further growth.

Getting the Relationship Blessed

When Sam asked Sarah and Bill why they wanted to be married in a church, they were taken aback by the question. After a pause, Sarah said, "I want a church wedding because it wouldn't seem like a real wedding if it wasn't in church." Bill agreed, "That's right, having a church wedding shows that you are serious about it, making your vows in front of God and everybody." After Sam asked them if there were any other reasons, they both admitted that their parents really wanted them to be married in church. Sam knew that both the couple and their parents were trying to say that a church wedding was the better way to get their marriage blessed.

The purpose of the wedding is to bless the marriage. It blesses the marriage in at least five different ways: (1) The couple chooses to get married to dedicate themselves to the relationship. Thus their participation in a wedding blesses the marriage in the *dedication* sense. (2) As a church service, it blesses the marriage, meaning it declares *God's and the church's approval* and conveys God's and the church's protection. (3) The wedding, when done according to the laws of the state, gives *the state's "blessing,"* which grants the couple a new legal status with the state's protection. (4) In the approval sense of blessing, *the family blesses* the festivities by participating in them and oftentimes contributing financially to them. (5) In the thanksgiving sense of the word *blessing,* family and friends bless by *celebrating the relationship* through the wedding and the various rituals and ceremonies that surround it.

Couples come to churches for a wedding out of an innate sense that weddings are profoundly religious events because they are about blessing. This is another reason for religious marriage preparation: Weddings are for blessing; they are religious events.

Caution Signs

If couples composed of previously unmarried individuals come for premarital guidance early in the process (before they have set a tentative date, or a long time before the tentative date they have set), or if such a couple wants to talk first about marriage or relationship instead of wedding, pastors should take them very seriously. This behavior is unusual enough to indicate that they know, sometimes only unconsciously, that there are important issues that need to be resolved before their psychological marriage can be completed. Such couples often need to do couple therapy before, along with, or instead of getting married.

Couples in which one (or both) of the partners has been previously married, such as Wilma and Rich, are more likely to sense a need to talk about marriage as well as weddings. Though these couples' concerns must be taken seriously, their willingness to seek counseling is not as big a caution sign as such willingness is among previously unmarried individuals.

Problems Getting the Family Blessing

Occasionally, parents or family members threaten to withhold their blessing because they object to the choice of mate or some other aspect of the wedding or marriage. According to family systems understandings (Friedman 1985, 166–67, 179–82), such situations usually indicate problems in the parents' marriage or the family member's (including the parents') relationship to their parents. Simply avoiding this situation by cutting the person off from the wedding, eloping, or placating does not work. These actions simply transfer the emotional intensity to the couple's marriage. Therefore, it is very important to work on these issues around the time of the wedding.

Fortunately, during the period surrounding the ceremony, family members are most willing to engage in the interactions that result in change. Their coming together for this ritual facilitates such interactions. When issues are worked through, the wedding blesses both the couple and the families of origin. (Good strategies for helping couples work with their families of origin are presented in Friedman 1985.) Otherwise, a session or two with a therapist specially trained in family therapy may be needed.

More frequently, couples worry that some small aspects of the wedding could cause family or friends to withhold their blessing. Couples need to know that uneasiness about these matters is natural for them and for their relatives. Friedman (1989, 125) tells us that when the family is relatively healthy, the couple's choices will cause only the normal upset that is a part of the marriage passage. If the family is not healthy, however, nothing the couple does about their choices will help. In this latter situation, dealing with the real relational issues in their family of origin is the only thing that will work.

Discerning Whom the Pastor Should Bless

Unfortunately, those accurately sensed and emotionally powerful complementary psychological traits that bring couples together will not, by themselves, hold couples together very long. For longevity in relationship, couples need three additional things: (1) shared values, (2) the willingness and the ability to leave and to cleave, and (3) communication and conflict-resolution skills. Therefore pastors should bless only those relationships that exhibit a sufficient amount of those three factors.

Because couples show their level of communication and conflict-resolution skills during the marriage-preparation sessions, the ability to handle the issues raised at that time provides a sufficient test of these skills. Likewise, the ability and willingness to engage in relationship shows itself in these sessions. Those partners who are not ready to leave old relationships (see below) because of immaturity, lukewarmness, grief, or entanglement probably should not be blessed. Likewise, those partners probably should not be blessed who show little aptitude for cleaving (see below). Finally, the amount of shared values can be measured by the amount of positive couple agreement on the eleven topics discussed in Chapter 3. Those with little positive couple agreement probably should not be blessed. As an alternative to not blessing these couples, their marriages can be blessed on the condition of participation in therapy and/or various other supportive activities such as workshops, marriage groups, special relationship with another couple, and ongoing participation in special groups and ministries.

Getting the relationship blessed is a multilayered process, not just a one-time event. One layer begins with family and friends approving and celebrating the engagement; another happens when a representative of the church (and state) hears and approves their story. The linking of couple's experiences and tasks with such "holy things" as the words of Scripture and the texts and rituals of the wedding ceremony during marriage preparation constitutes a third and profound layer of blessing. These three layers support, deepen, and add to the emotional effectiveness of the fourth and most visible layer of blessing, the wedding itself.

Not all couples are like Jacob, willing to wrestle all night to get a blessing (Gen. 32:24-28). Some do not wish to spend the time it takes to explore their story with a pastor or counselor. Others refuse to share themselves when they do spend the time. A few are too opposed to the pastor's religion to try linking their experiences and tasks with Scripture, liturgies, and ritual acts. When pastors interview such persons, they have to decide whether or not to invest their time and energy in working with them.

Though God blesses whom God wills, the full, glorious emotional *experience* of God's blessing is usually linked to engaging in Jacob-like activities, that is, the willingness to wrestle all night with issues and angels, sacrificing the time and bearing the pain that leads to a new name. Therefore, pastors must ask themselves questions about the couples' willingness to participate in the premarital guidance process: Are they willing enough to wrestle that I am willing to participate in declaring their marriage blessed? Or is their engagement in the process so low that my marrying them will be collaborating with their avoidance?

Summary of Blessing

Couples come to pastors to discuss the wedding because they have already begun their psychological marriage. They need a wedding to get a blessing from the church, state, family, and friends. Because their psychological marriage is based on a profound experience of discovery and driven by powerful feelings and hormones, it is hard to stop. Pastors can take some consolation from the knowledge that the couple's choice of mate is most likely accurate in terms of the psychological characteristics with which they need to struggle. Yet because longevity in relationship depends on shared values, the ability and willingness to leave and cleave, and communication and conflict-resolution skills, pastors should determine the presence of these factors before blessing a relationship. The process of experiencing the full marriage blessing involves exploring their story and linking it with the wedding liturgy. Pastors have to decide what level of couple participation in that process warrants their own investment of time and energy.

LEAVING

The wedding ritual declares and enables the partners' decision to leave or revise their old relationships. This ritual and the marriage license give the church's and state's permission to create a new family. Participation in the ceremony by the partners' family members conveys their consent to this modification of relationships. After the wedding, the new spouses legally become each other's closest family member, changing forever their relationships with the members of their families of origin.

Although the wedding celebrates the couple's passage from their families of origin to their new family, the ritual itself does not accomplish this relational change. Rabbi Friedman (1989, 124) makes this point well: "Ceremonies celebrate. From an emotional systems point of view, they are not in themselves efficacious. Rather their effect is determined by what has already been developing within the emotional system of the family." Therefore, couples need to begin leaving and cleaving during the premarital period to participate fully in their wedding (and marriage).

The necessity of leaving in order to cleave applies to all couples. It is most apparent with persons who have never physically left home. Their emotional and financial dependence on their families of origin is obvious. Yet many who are residentially emancipated, like Rich, are still emotionally dependent. Rich talks over everything with his mother first; Myrtle always knows what Rich is thinking and feeling. Even those who have residential, financial, and considerable emotional independence, like Sarah, carry their family of origin within themselves as models of male and female relationships. Sarah's models must be revised so that she and Bill can relate as they are and not as her images dictate. Whether a person is dependent on his or her family of origin on all levels or just carries images from them, all persons have to revise their relationship with their family of origin in order to create a new family.

In addition to families of origin, many partners have other families to leave in order to cleave. Like many who are relatively independent of their families of origin, Sarah has developed intense friendships as her "family of support"; she has two girlfriends with whom she discusses everything. Both Wilma and Rich have families of decision: She has an ex-husband and two minor children; he has an ex-wife. Relationships with families of support and families of decision have to be revised in the same way as relationships with families of origin. All persons entering marriage have familial relationships that they must leave, in some degree, in order to cleave to their new partner.

Children and Leaving

Partners who have children pose a special problem for revising relationships. On the one hand, their responsibility for the children cannot be reduced in the way other familial relationships can, but on the other hand, the marriage will be compromised if one partner does not make the other partner primary. The fact that children usually do not want their parents to make their partners primary makes the situation even more difficult. The final complication comes from the continuing need to relate to the children's other parent.

Wilma brought these problems with changing relationships to her union with Rich. Her daughters resented the time that she spent with Rich and they acted it out. Sheila, 10, the oldest, continued to try to reunite Wilma with Henry, her father. Terry, 7, cried every time her mother went out with Rich, and she began doing poorly in school. Henry didn't help, either; when he had the children for a weekend, he grilled them about Rich. In addition, Henry became irregular with child support; he explained this new behavior by saying that Wilma had gotten herself another "meal ticket." Wilma was distraught by all this confusion; she loved her daughters and wanted them to share in the happiness that she was experiencing.

Dr. Washington knew that persons entering marriage with divorces and children need special attention and time to work on changing relationships. Therefore she negotiated with Wilma and Rich for individual sessions to talk with each about their former marriages and what they learned from them.

Cultural Differences in Leaving

Appropriate leaving differs among various racial or ethnic groups and social classes because of their variation in family models. For instance, many middle-class white Anglo-Saxon Protestant (WASP) families, like Bill's, support autonomy by the couple and define the family as the nuclear family (the parents and children). Conversely, Sarah's Italian-American family expects less autonomy and defines the family as the extended family, which includes grandparents, aunts and uncles, cousins, in-laws, godparents, and some neighbors, as well as parents and children (Rotunno and McGoldrick 1982). Similarly, many African American families, like Rich's, define themselves to include grandparents, aunts, uncles, cousins, in-laws, certain church members, as well as parents and children (Hines and Boyd-Franklin 1982). Blue-collar black families, like Rich's, often expect the new family to help other members of the extended family.

Because middle-class WASPs set the style in the United States, members of other subcultures often find themselves torn between the WASP family model and their own. This struggle between models was a problem for Rich and his former wife, Helen. As the oldest child, and a male, Rich believed he had an ongoing and high-priority responsibility to help his parents, siblings, and other members of his extended family. This subcultural pattern became dear to Rich when he saw how much his grandmothers, parents, uncles, and aunts sacrificed to help him become the first college graduate in the family. Helen came from a middle-class black family; both of her parents had advanced degrees, and three of her grandparents were college graduates. Helen and her parents, who had adopted the nuclear family model, never approved of the time and money Rich spent helping his family of origin.

Differences in models for changing of relationships is one of the factors that complicates marriages across racial, ethnic, or class lines. It is important for pastors to be cognizant of cultural differences, so that they do not assume that the needed leaving can or should look the same for all couples.

Leaving as a Step of Faith

The process of leaving one's family can be described as the beginning of a religious journey. Anderson and Mitchell (1993, 134–35) describe leaving home as a "religious act." Leaving is inspired by a religious revelation (the experience of the beloved), and moves toward the blessing of a deeper union with the beloved.

Leaving, like the experience of the Holy, has elements of both fear and fascination. Part of each partner is excited by the new possibilities. It is this exhilaration and joy that invites people to leave the old, and it sustains them on the journey. Another part of them, often suppressed, is terrified at leaving the known for the unknown. To leave one's old relations, no matter how problematic they are, requires stepping out into the unknown supported by nothing but faith. To base one's future on the unknown, no matter how promising, means swinging out over the abyss supported only by gossamer threads of hope. Thus couples frequently experience acute bouts of doubts and fears prior to the wedding.

The Christian heritage has many images of leaving as a journey of faith. Anderson and Mitchell (1993, 135) use the image of Abram being called out of the land Ur (Gen. 12:1ff) to characterize leaving home. Other similar biblical images of leaving are the children of Israel leaving Egypt (Exod. 14:1ff), and Jesus being driven by the Spirit into the wilderness to be tempted (Matt. 4:1ff). Each of these journeys was inspired by a revelation and each was taken in order to receive a blessing. Abram, who experienced God in a vision, was called out of Haran to receive the blessing of being the father of a new people (Gen. 12:1ff). Moses, who experienced God in the burning bush (Exod.3:3ff), was called out of Egypt to receive the blessing of a new land. Jesus was called from baptismal bliss into the desert to receive the blessing of a clarified and empowered vocation (Matt. 3:16-17). God called Abram, Moses, and Jesus to leave the old in order to receive a blessing in the new. The call to marriage is a call to leave the old relationships to receive a greater blessing in the new relationship.

Leaving Is Not Running Away

Some partners attempt to marry as a way of escaping an oppressive or unhealthy family system. Their drive to marry relates more to their own search for freedom than to their partner's viability as a spouse. Some of these persons can be identified by their sense of urgency about getting married. Others show a desire to cut their families out of the ceremonies. Many can be detected by the partner's obvious inappropriateness as a spouse because of abuse, addiction, lack of responsibility, or low couple agreement on the marriage-preparation topics.

Paradoxically, the way to leave an unhealthy family system involves engaging it. This insight can be stated as follows: "If you do not deal with your family, you take its dysfunction with you." The emotional independence and maturity needed to reorder relationships comes, in part, from dealing with the difficult relationships in one's own family. Another part comes from experience in exercising one's own judgment and meeting one's needs.

Some Are Not Ready to Leave

In some cases one or both partners are not ready to revise their relationships because of youth or immaturity. People who have not yet demonstrated the ability to live independently sometimes attempt to get married as a premature bid for independence. Other such persons are forced by their parents or partner to consider marriage because of pregnancy.

Persons with some maturity may consider marriage as an escape from isolation or pain. Even though they do not feel a strong attraction for their partner, some persons seek marriage because it is expected by society or seems a cure for loneliness.

Other relatively mature persons may seek to marry while they are still grieving a divorce or a death. Such persons—Wilma and Rich, for example—were not sufficiently emotionally free from the old relationships to revise them easily. Partners seeking escape from pain or grief can be identified by either their lukewarmness or their strange intensity. Another indication is that less than two years have elapsed between a divorce or the death of a spouse and the anticipated wedding. Still another is the energy (blaming or adoration) with which they refer to their previous partner.

Such immature, lonely, or grieving persons are not ready to do the revising of relationships that is necessary for marriage. Therefore, pastors should follow Dr. Washington's example and try to encourage such persons to work on these issues before they marry. A few sessions with a therapist trained in family therapy is often needed for those still not disengaged from their families. Grief work with therapists, grief groups, and divorce healing groups are indicated for those still grieving. Lonely people may need to deal with their own loneliness through therapy before they deal with another's loneliness. If such people refuse the referral, the pastor probably should not participate in their wedding.

Leaving Comes before Wedding

The need to change relationships begins in the premarital period. Couples start to demand exclusiveness of each other and make plans with each other and for each other. Likewise, they begin to share feelings and thoughts with each other that they have not shared with others. Couples have to wrestle with the allotment of time and resources to families of origin and support and, if applicable, families of decision. The process of planning a wedding forces the couple to change relationships as they decide what kind of wedding they are going to have, where it is to be, whom to invite, who is to make up the bridal party and altar party, what kind of reception to have, and for how many. These decisions invariably involve going against some family or peer group traditions, limiting the influence of some family members and friends, and taking care of some of the couple's wants and needs first.

The changing of the relationship happens through partners taking small concrete actions that put the partner first. One example of such actions was Rich telling his parents that Wilma came first, so he would have to miss working in their yard one Saturday in order to take care of something with her. Wilma came to grips with the fact that she was putting Rich first when she, with Dr. Washington's help, decided not to force her daughters to be part of the bridal party, thus acknowledging that the wedding was for her and not the three of them. Each of these small actions changed the person's previous familial relationships by putting the partner first. The revising of relationships takes place through these kinds of concrete decisions and actions.

Summary of Leaving

Partners must change their old relationships so that they can create a new marital relationship. That is, they must leave in order to cleave. Without such changing, partners' old families of origin, support, and decision will interfere with this new creation by limiting the special intimacies and exclusive choices that feed the couple's relationship. Each partner must deal with his or her own family in order to leave constructively. Eloping, cutting off the family, or placating the family do not work. The emotional intensity left unresolved with the family transfers to the marital relationship and poisons it.

Leaving begins a journey in faith like the biblical journeys of Abram, Moses, and Jesus. It begins before marriage and takes place through small concrete actions. Leaving is a journey inspired by the foretaste of blessing that brought the couple together, and it moves toward a more glorious blessing that is promised for the future.

CLEAVING

Cleaving is the purpose for leaving. The whole premarital and wedding process moves toward cleaving: building the marriage relationship. The psychological marriage begins this relationship by declaring it exclusive, and the wedding makes it official. Yet couples preparing for marriage have to employ their time, talent, and treasure to construct the frame on which their relationship will be built. Mutually agreed-upon roles, rules, and rituals constitute that frame.

Cleaving differs from leaving in that partners leave individually but they cleave collaboratively. Thus, building a marriage relationship involves partners assigning each other roles; agreeing on the rules for relating to each other, their possessions, and other people; and developing ritual ways to spend their time, talent, and treasure. The couple builds this frame during the premarital and early marriage periods both by conscious decisions and by conscious and unconscious patterns of interaction.

Sarah and Bill showed one of their sets of rules, roles, and rituals for relating to each other during the opening session, in which Sarah initiated much of the conversation. She leaned forward, started a subject, and information and opinions poured out of her. When she finished, she turned to Bill for confirmation. Bill in the meantime had been leaning back quietly, seemingly disengaged from the conversation. After she finished, he responded. Bill and Sarah exercise their power differently in their verbal interactions during the premarital conferences: She uses her power to initiate, he uses his to veto or affirm, and she accepts his response as theirs. She is conscious of this interactional pattern or ritual and he is not. They have an implicit rule against direct conflict that governs their discussions about social needs and their interactions in the premarital guidance sessions.

Marriage in Transition

The contemporary societal transition from hierarchical marriage to companionship marriage complicates the process of cleaving. The hierarchical marriage was developed to meet the need for order in society and the survival of the partners and the species. By contrast, the contemporary companionship marriage places the feelings of the individual partners about their relationship at the center and trusts other arrangements for society's order and survival.

Hierarchical marriage. The chief purposes of the traditional marriage were to provide children for the population of society and to ensure that the children were legitimate for the orderly assignment of property, rights, and relationships. Marriage established kinship between families, knitting them together into larger units that contributed to the society's political stability. The families created by these marriages were productive economic units that owned or worked farms or businesses or trades as units and passed on skills as families. They were also cultural units that passed on the myths, rituals, knowledge, and artifacts of the society. The extended family, church, and state overtly dictated many of the roles, rules, and rituals of these familial units that were so important to the society's political, economic, and cultural order and survival. For instance, society expected the husband to be in charge; all property (including the bride) was put in his name, and he alone was allowed to vote. In this hierarchical marriage, the wife was expected to follow the husband's direction, cook, clean, raise children, and help on the farm or in the business.

Sarah's family of origin is in this traditional hierarchical mold. Her father, John (Giovanni was his birth name, but he anglicized it), was the unquestioned head of the family. He worked hard in the coal mines and on the little family farm to provide for the family. Sarah's mother, Maria, cooked, cleaned, took care of the six children, and raised a small garden. John, a quiet man, really loved the family. He expected, however, to be obeyed by the children and have his edicts supported by his wife. He taught the four boys to farm and insisted that they stay in school so that they wouldn't have to work in the mines as he did.

Sarah, John's youngest child, was the apple of his eye. They both loved it when he would read to her. She wanted to farm with him, but he insisted that she help her mother in the house and learn to cook and clean "like a girl should." He also saw that they were a faithful Roman Catholic family that attended mass every Sunday and participated in the feast days and church programs. When Sarah became a teenager and started questioning the authority of her father and the church, John was deeply troubled by what he felt was disloyal defiance.

Companionship marriage. The companionship marriage differs significantly from the traditional marriage; its chief purpose is the mutual joy of the partners. Neither additional population nor the orderly transmission of property through family lines is necessary for the survival of contemporary American society. Further, the state does not need associations of related families to hold it together. In contemporary society most families are simply consumers; businesses take care of economic production; schools and other organizations provide cultural transmission. Thus in this present situation, marriage meets relational needs more than societal requirements.

In this new situation, the society dictates far fewer roles, rules, and rituals. Thus, couples like Bill and Sarah have to decide whether they will take Bill's last name, combine the two last names, or keep their individual last names. They have to decide who cooks, who cleans, and who manages the property. They have to decide whether to open Christmas gifts on Christmas Eve after Midnight Mass like her family or on Christmas morning like his. Like one of Bill's good friends, they could agree not to give gifts to each other and contribute the money they save to helping the poor. Because they have to make these decisions together, it is very important that there be considerable positive couple agreement about the marriage-preparation topics in companionship marriage. Companionship couples need a strong foundation of agreement to stand on as they make decisions in the areas on which they either disagree or about which they hadn't thought before. They also need considerable communication and conflict-resolution skills to work on all of these decisions.

The Transition and Cleaving

This transition from hierarchical to companionship marriage complicates the process of cleaving in several ways. First, many people have grown up in families with hierarchical marriages and have these images deep within them, luring them or frightening them or both. Sarah may well long for Bill to give her the strong, quiet comfort her father, as undisputed head of the household, could give her as a child. Yet she would be very much afraid that allowing Bill the power her father had would result in his ignoring her wants, as she felt her father did to her mother.

Second, the roles, rules, and rituals for companionship marriage are still in the experimental stage in our society. Thus the couple cannot get much tried-and-true guidance in beginning a companionship marriage. Bill might wonder what is the appropriate amount of cooking and cleaning for him to do, since Sarah is so much better at it. On the one hand, he would want to be fair. Yet, on the other hand, he would need the extra time to put into his job. That is because both he and Sarah would want him to be the primary breadwinner, so that they can afford for her to stay home for a while when they have children. Bill wishes he knew what the accepted formula was for these situations, or at least whom to ask for it. Sarah has similar questions.

Cleaving differs in hierarchical and companionship marriages. A good part of cleaving in the traditional marriage involves clinging to the institution of marriage and carrying out society's roles. Sarah's father, John, cleaved by being the breadwinner and leader of the household. Her mother, Maria, cleaved by being the mother of his children and supporting his leadership. The companionship marriage has the opposite model of cleaving. In it the partners concentrate on joining a particular person, not a role. Thus Sarah and Bill depend totally on the quality of their relationship and the depth of their agreements on the important topics to keep them together.

In the traditional hierarchical marriage, "role competence," the ability to master the roles assigned to a person by society, was the key to marital stability and happiness. That is why Sarah's father, John, was so insistent on Sarah learning the things "that a girl should." He wanted her to be happy and successful in marriage. The companionship marriage relies on "relational competence," skill in communication and conflict resolution. Bill and Sarah need these skills to work out roles, rules, and rituals that make them happy and the relationship successful.

Likewise, in the traditional marriage, "rule acceptance," the willingness to follow the rules of church and society, were the foundation for strong and healthy marriages. That is why Sarah's father was so upset when she began to question his and the church's authority. In the companionship marriage, "shared values," positive couple agreement in many key marital areas, provides the basis for good marriages; thus arises the correlation between considerable positive couple agreement on the marriage-preparation topics and happiness and longevity in marriage.

Cleaving as Bonding in the Desert

If leaving can be described as similar to the exodus of the children of Israel from Egypt, then cleaving approximates the Israelites becoming a people in the desert in preparation for receiving the blessing of a new land (cf. Exod. 15:22—20, and the book of Deuteronomy). Learning to communicate and resolve conflicts with a new partner is analogous to the journey of the Israelites through the wilderness looking for signs, rules, food, and water as they learned to cleave to God and to one another (Exod. 15–20). Just as the Israelites often wanted to return to slavery rather than endure the hardships of the wilderness (Exod. 16:3, 17:3), a couple beginning the process of cleaving has periods of wishing for the old certainties, no matter how problematic they were.

During the time in the desert there was much conflict among the people of Israel (Exod. 15:22ff, 16:2ff, 17:1ff). Yet it was through these conflicts that they learned about God's grace and forged their identity as a nation. It was through resolving these conflicts that they became a people ready to enter the promised land. Similarly, couples engage in much conflict as they attempt to cleave to each other, yet these conflicts can be the key to both self-understanding and to developing their identity as a couple. The resolution of conflicts prepares them for the blessing of their "promised land" of a deeper, more satisfying union.

As the Israelites wandered through the wilderness, they discovered God's power to bless. They learned that God could give them water from the rock (Exod. 17:6-7), food from the sky (Exod. 16:13ff), and commandments on the mountain (Exod. 19, 20). Just as in the biblical story, delightful discoveries appear as the couple "bonds in the wilderness"— solutions where they thought there were none, comfort in the midst of the hardest situations, and new rules that organize their common life in satisfying ways. Thus couples discover God's power to bless on the way to receiving a greater blessing.

Difficulties with Cleaving

Cleaving is difficult for many people because it involves both the freedom and the skills to engage in intense conflict resolution. There are several circumstances that limit people's freedom. It is hard, if not impossible, for those who are not ready to leave because they have either cut off all ties with their families or placated them and thus have not become healthily independent of them. Such persons need to work through these issues with their families of origin. People who have not resolved their grief over the death of or their divorce from a previous spouse are not ready to cleave; nor are those persons who are unusually set in their ways or have great difficulty working collaboratively. Watching the interaction between partners in premarital interviews is a way to identify persons of this latter type. Couples with little positive agreement on the topics discussed in Chapter 3 comprise still another group that experiences great difficulty with cleaving. Couples in these groups should undertake couple counseling before, with, or instead of the wedding.

Research (Gottman 1994; Markmann et al. 1994) indicates that the most important conflict-resolution skill is that of engaging in the conflict. Conversely, the most relationship-damaging response to conflict is withdrawal from it or avoidance of it. An important conflict-resolution skill is communicating respect for the other person, as opposed to criticizing or invalidating her or him. Another conflict-resolution skill is decreasing conflict with nondefensive responses to one's partner's complaints or criticisms instead of escalating conflict through defensive replies. Finally, developing the skill of positive or neutral interpretation of your partner's thoughts and actions, instead of negative interpretations, aids in successful conflict resolution.

Watching the interaction between partners during premarital interviews is a way to identify people who have difficulty cleaving. Attempts to teach couples conflict-resolution skills usually help the pastor to discern between those couples who are not free to engage in conflict and those who are simply unskilled. The latter make much more progress in learning the skills than the former.

Fr. Sam attempted to teach Sarah and Bill conflict-resolution skills by having them talk through their conflicts, facing each other, in his presence. He stopped them to point out conversational sequences that exhibited a lack of conflict-resolution skills. Then he had them discuss their feelings about these sequences. Next he had them brainstorm ways conflict-resolution skills could have been used in the sequence under discussion. Finally he had them redo the sequence using the skills this time. After doing this several times during the session, Sarah and Bill's conflict-resolution skills showed notable improvement, and they were excited about that development.

Practicing Cleaving

The whole process of wedding planning forced Sarah and Bill to do much intense communication and conflict resolution as they made decisions about the marriage service. During this process, Fr. Sam helped them to look at their patterns of interaction and their methods of resolving conflicts, so that they were able to make more conscious decisions about how they wanted to engage in cleaving.

Summary of Cleaving

Building a new relationship requires strong communication and conflict-resolution skills because the couple has to work out ways to meet their complementary needs and unite their diverse backgrounds in mutually satisfying roles, rules, and rituals. The current state of transition between hierarchical and companionship marriage means that there are few roles, rules, and rituals for the couple simply to adopt. This lack of models and guidelines makes the process of building a marriage relationship even more complex. Thus the importance of a strong foundation of positive couple agreement on the marriage-preparation topics to support the partners as they invent their marriage.

The religious dimension of cleaving reveals itself in the similarities between the experiences of couples who are cleaving and the experiences of the Israelites bonding in the desert: much conflict in the midst of which come wondrous experiences of God. All of the activities of premarital guidance create opportunities for identifying couples' strengths and weaknesses in relational skills and positive couple agreement. The activity of wedding planning, however, provides particularly good opportunities for practicing conflict resolution and cleaving.

CONCLUSION OF COMMON TASKS
AND THEIR RELIGIOUS FOUNDATIONS

Couples face three basic tasks in the period before marriage: blessing, leaving, and cleaving. These tasks are so compelling that they drive these couples' activities and interactions. Because the wedding provides the occasion for working on these tasks, one can understand all of the energy, care, and emotionality that coalesce around wedding arrangements. Likewise, knowing that couples and families are struggling with these basic tasks when they discuss arrangement details helps one to understand how seemingly minor points can result in so much anxiety, conflict, and guilt. Further, lack of readiness for these tasks is an indication of lack of readiness for marriage. Thus pastors should not bless such unions without the couple engaging in professional individual, couple, or family counseling.

Because these three tasks each have a religious dimension, analogies can be drawn between them and key biblical stories: for example, between the experience of bonding and the experience of God's blessing of Adam and Eve as parts of each other; between leaving one's family and friends and Abram leaving Ur, the Israelites leaving Egypt, and Jesus in the desert; finally, between cleaving and the Israelites bonding in the desert. The striking success of religious couples in cleaving (Filsinger and Wilson 1984; Greeley 1980, 1991), the purpose of blessing and leaving, supports the premise that these three tasks are religious. This religious dimension of the tasks links them to the pastoral resources.

Religious traditions offer the partners stories and practices that sustain the hope that anxiety cries for, the absolution for which guilt longs, and the love that grows through conflict. The religious resources put the troublesome details of preparing for a wedding in the larger context of faith, thus removing their sting. Though pastors may use psychological resources to understand the tasks or to help couples complete them, their primary and unique resources are religious wisdom and practice.

5

TEACHING
SCRIPTURE PASTORALLY

Scripture constitutes a major pastoral resource for helping couples deal with their issues and tasks in preparing for marriage. Scripture teaches the law and the gospel, challenges the unhelpful beliefs that underlie many issues and unmet needs, and, most important, Scripture guides couples into more helpful perspectives from which to view these issues and meet these needs.

Teaching Scripture as a pastoral resource involves using the skills and methods, which were discussed in the previous chapters, for applying the Bible to couples' issues and tasks. The proclamation skills of informing, sharing, contending, and reviewing constitute the central skills for teaching Scripture. Informing involves communicating needed information and correcting harmful misinformation. Informing differs from academic teaching in three ways: (1) It is focused on one of the parishioner's beliefs, (2) it responds to the parishioner's need, and (3) it deals with feelings as well as ideas. Sharing consists of offering a portion of the pastor's experiences to the parishioners. Contending means to dispute a parishioner's beliefs by using reason and religious resources. Reviewing involves inviting parishioners to summarize their understandings after they have been challenged. The use of pastoral skills and methods makes pastoral teaching a type of pastoral care.

This chapter shows how Ephesians 5:21-33, a passage of Scripture that has been a primary text for the discussion of marriage throughout Christian history, can be used to deal pastorally with couples' issues. The discussion follows this order: (1) the background of the conversation, (2) a conversation illustrating the pastoral teaching of this passage, (3) a reflection on the skills and methods the pastor uses in the conversation, (4) a new exegesis of this familiar passage to support Dr. Washington's particular interpretation of the text, and (5) finally, the implications of this passage for modern marriage.

DR. WASHINGTON, RICH, AND WILMA STUDY EPHESIANS

When Wilma, Rich, and Dr. Washington met for the Scripture session, the couple had finished the *Growing Together* course, their two individual sessions, and their couple session with Dr. Washington. In the first of these sessions Dr. Washington had helped Wilma see that her lack of assertiveness had contributed to her problems with her former husband. In the third session, when Wilma and Rich met to discuss their individual sessions, Wilma had asked Rich to support her in using more direct communication. During this session Dr. Washington led them in doing the Assertive Communication exercise in the Prepare/Enrich booklet. Dr. Washington noticed that Wilma had become more assertive in the *Growing Together* class, but she knew that learning a different style of communication requires a lot of practice and a lot of support, both personal and conceptual.

As a black Baptist, Dr. Washington was committed to teaching from Scripture, a commitment that was constantly renewed by the peculiar vibrancy of scriptural words and images in the African American community. Yet as a black preacher she exercised the freedom to interpret Scripture creatively in order to teach its central truths. She claimed the liberty that the slaves took when they ignored the white preachers' sermons on "slaves obey your . . . masters," (Eph. 6:5) because they knew that the central message of Scripture supported their liberation. Thus Dr. Washington chose the Ephesians text, so that the biblical passage that had supported Wilma's oppression could be redeemed to support her new assertiveness.

Initial Concerns

Before they had a chance to sit down, Rich said, "Dr. Washington, Wilma and I are really glad that we are finally going to talk about the biblical guidelines for marriage." Years of training had taught her to explore a statement like that; so she probed: "What are you concerned about, Rich?" Rich replied, "Wilma and I have been talking about what Christian marriage would be like, because we don't want to have the same kind of marriages we had before. We want to get it right this time." "Get it right?" asked Dr. Washington. "Yes," Rich responded, "we want a relationship that is based on God's word, so that it will last."

Noticing that Wilma had been silent, Dr. Washington looked toward her as if to ask what she thought. Wilma took the cue and said, "Rich and I want a marriage with a solid spiritual foundation. Rich is not like Henry, who wouldn't even go to church with me, just sat at home and watched football. Henry would say, 'Woman, Sunday is my day off!' So we've been wondering if there is a biblical understanding of marriage to get Rich and me started right . . . something except that Ephesians thing that they taught at that backwards church where I used to go." "Ephesians thing?" asked Dr. Washington. "You know," replied Wilma, "the man being the head and the wife obeying and all that out-of-date stuff that I have no intention of doing and I know that you don't do, either."

Dr. Washington offered a summary: "As I understand it, the two of you really want guidance for establishing a marriage that is based on biblical understandings because you believe these will make it more permanent than your previous relationships. Is that right?" Rich immediately said, "Yes," but Wilma added, "as long as it deals with contemporary understandings about men and women."

Expanding Their Understandings

"Fair enough," replied the pastor, who then looked at Wilma, smiled, and said, "if you are willing to look at Ephesians." Still looking at Wilma, she said, "You are right. I don't understand my husband as boss, and I don't obey as if I were his servant or something. But that is not what the passage is about. It has a beautiful message about mutuality in marriage that has been so grossly misunderstood that it was worth taking Greek in seminary so that I could appreciate it."

Dr. Washington concluded with a challenge: "Wilma, are you willing to look at this passage with me for an hour and a half and then tell me what you think about it?" Wilma nodded and said, "I'll try," without much conviction. She turned to Rich and inquired, "What about you, Rich?" Rich looked at Wilma and said, "I'm willing to look at it, but Wilma's right, it has to speak to our relationship, because we treat each other with respect."

Introducing the passage. The pastor responded, "It sounds to me that the both of you are still a little uneasy about Ephesians because you think it will go contrary to the mutuality that you have." Both nodded their heads in agreement. Dr. Washington continued, "I can understand your concern, because this passage is frequently used to support the patriarchal marriage that people like you are moving away from. However, it clearly says the very opposite. Let's look at it and see what it really says." She moved beside them, opened her New Revised Standard Bible, and showed them the following passage from Ephesians 5:

> 21. Be subject to one another out of reverence for Christ. 22. Wives, be subject to your husbands as you are to the Lord. 23. For the husband is the head of the wife just as Christ is the head of the church, the body of which he is the Savior. 24. Just as the church is subject to Christ, so also wives

ought to be, in everything, to their husbands. 25. Husbands, love your wives, just as Christ loved the church and gave himself up for her, 26. in order to make her holy by cleansing her with the washing of water by the word, 27. so as to present the church to himself in splendor, without a spot or wrinkle or anything of the kind—yes, so that she may be holy and without blemish. 28. In the same way, husbands should love their wives as they do their own bodies. He who loves his wife loves himself. 29. For no one ever hates his own body, but he nourishes and tenderly cares for it, just as Christ does for the church, 30. because we are members of his body. 31. "For this reason a man will leave his father and mother and be joined to his wife, and the two will become one flesh." 32. This is a great mystery, and I am applying it to Christ and the church. 33. Each of you, however, should love his wife as himself, and a wife should respect her husband.

Dr. Washington began, "Notice the first verse, 'Be subject to one another out of reverence for Christ.' 'Be subject to one another' establishes the theme of mutuality for the whole passage. It does not begin with wives being subject, but with both being subject to each other. Mutual subjection is Paul's understanding of the new way that Christians are to act toward each other. He applies this to wives and husbands in this passage, children and parents in chapter 6 verses 1-4, and slaves and masters in chapter 6 verses 5-9. People misunderstand this whole passage when they begin it with verse 22, 'Wives, be subject to your husbands. . . .' and not verse 21 'Be subject to one another. . . .' Do you see what I mean?" Yes, I kind of see what you mean about mutual subjection, but it still says wives are to be subject in verse 22 and it doesn't say anything about husbands being subject," countered Wilma.

"Be subject" parallels love. Dr. Washington smiled and said, "That bothered me too when I first read the passage. I couldn't see where it was mutual until I understood that the instruction in verse 25, 'Husbands, love your wives. . . .' is the parallel to 'Wives, be subject to your husbands. . . .' Now, I know 'be subject' and 'love' don't sound a lot alike in English but remember that the New Testament wasn't written in English, it was written in Greek, and the meanings of 'be subject' and 'love' are very similar in that language. Are you with me?"

"We're listening," replied Rich. "Keep going," said Wilma. "I am glad that you are with me, because we are getting to the difficult part now," the pastor continued. "The word translated 'be subject' means voluntarily to renounce one's will for the sake of the other. It is something that is done between equals. Being subject is like a gift you give to someone, it's not something someone forces you to do. The fact that it's a voluntary action is hard to say in English, but it's what the Greek means. Does that make any sense to you?

"You mean, pastor, that my obeying my husband is a gift I give and not a right he can demand?" responded Wilma. "Yes, that is exactly what I mean; your cooperation is a gift, not a right, because the two of you are equals," confirmed Dr. Washington. Then she continued, "But *obey* is too strong a word. Being subject means 'give way to one another' (Jerusalem Bible 1966), '"Fit in with" each other' (J. B. Phillips 1972), 'support each other' (Barth 1974), 'sacrifice for each other' (Eph. 5:25). Your husband is as bound to cooperate with you as you with him. In fact, the passage addresses the husband's need to sacrifice or submit much more than it does the wife. We will get to that part soon."

Wilma perked up, "Wow, that's sounding much better." "I'm glad that it's sounding better to you, Wilma," the pastor replied, "because that is what it means." Suddenly, Wilma looked pained again. "I like the way you are going, pastor, and I don't mean to be rude, but I'm still waiting to hear more about how 'being subject' is the same as 'love.'"

Dealing with feelings. Dr. Washington said gently, "Wilma, this passage is difficult for you, isn't it?" Wilma mumbled, "Yes." The pastor continued, "Have you been hurt by this passage?" Wilma blurted:

> "I tried so hard to be a good Christian wife like Reverend Johnson taught at Ebeneezer Baptist Church. I tried to treat Henry as the head of the house. I tried to submit. Pastor, you don't know how hard I tried . . . time and time again, I'd try . . . and things wouldn't work out . . . and I'd go to the pastor or to some of the 'church mothers' [respected senior women] . . . and they'd tell me that if I 'followed God's word,' everything would be right . . . they'd throw this passage at me . . . throw it at me . . . never at Henry . . . just at me! I tried so hard . . . it hurt so bad . . . and things never got right!"

Wilma stopped, with tears running down her cheeks.

After a long pause, Wilma pulled herself together and continued, "Dr. Washington, I didn't mean to interrupt your teaching with an outburst, but when you mentioned my hurt, it just came out." The pastor replied softly, "I'm glad it came out, honey; it was important that you express your feelings." "But I didn't want to cause any trouble," Wilma sniffled. The pastor asked sternly, "Wilma, did you hear what I just said?" Wilma replied, "You mean about it being important for me to express my feelings?" "Yes." "But it's embarrassing for me to go to pieces while you are trying to teach." "Wilma, your feelings are so important that my teaching won't be of much help to you and Rich unless you express them, just like you did." "OK, pastor," Wilma continued, "if its all right with you." "How are you feeling now, Wilma?" asked Dr. Washington. Wilma responded, "I'm feeling a little better now that I've got that off my chest and you know how I feel about this passage."

Anger. The pastor continued, "Is there more you need to say, Wilma?" Wilma answered, "Well, it's not Christian, but I am upset with Reverend Johnson and especially those women for telling me that stuff." "Upset," Dr. Washington reflected. Wilma went on, "Yeah, telling me all that submission junk when I needed help was just awful; it really steams me to think of all that I went through." "Sounds like you are angry," the pastor rejoined. "I know that Christians are supposed to forgive and forget, but I can't make my feelings act right. I still don't like Reverend Johnson and those women—that's why I left Ebeneezer and came to GMZ," Wilma retorted.

"Wilma, your anger is very important to both your Christian walk and to your preparation for marriage; I'm glad you are sharing it." "OK, pastor." "Well, I mean it, Wilma; you can't engage in mutual self-giving or love if you withhold your anger. Sharing your anger is self-giving. It lets the other person know what the issues are so the two of you can work on them. Does that make sense to you?" "Kind of. It's as if the other person can't help if they don't know there's a problem." "That's what I meant, Wilma." "Pastor, I feel a lot better now, I'm ready to go on."

Review. "Before we go on, this is a good time to review what you have understood so far. Rich what have you learned?" Dr. Washington asked as she focused on him. "Well, pastor, you told us that this Scripture is about mutuality, husband and wife working together to help each other, not about the man ruling the wife like the old folks used to say. And I learned that Wilma is mad about the way they taught her this passage at Ebeneezer."

"And you," the pastor said, turning her gaze to Wilma. Wilma responded, "As Rich said, you showed us that this passage begins by talking about mutuality. The wife's cooperation is a gift, not a duty. . . . And I am upset about being forced to obey as a duty. I feel better about this passage now, but I still want to hear more about how 'cooperate' and 'love' are the same thing."

The pastor pressed her, "Did you learn anything else, Wilma?" After a long pause came a soft reply: "I learned that it's all right with you if I express my anger." "Well," Dr. Washington began, "I wanted to you to learn a little more than that. I wanted you to understand that sharing your anger is important for your working together with Rich. The two of you won't be able to do things mutually if you don't let him know what makes you angry. That's what I wanted you to hear."

After a pause, Wilma said softly, "That's hard for me to accept. I have always been told that anger isn't Christian. And I have always tried to be a good Christian." Wilma and Dr. Washington talked a little more about anger and its importance in the Christian life and in marriage.

Summary of the remainder of the lesson. Dr. Washington continued the Scripture lesson by asking Wilma and Rich to personalize the issues in the text by identifying situations in which they practiced mutual self-giving and support well, and situations in which they had difficulty with mutuality. Next, she asked each one to tell the other what particular needs for respect or nurture he or she had, when the other had met their needs, and when the other had not met those needs.

Negotiating a Contract

After having each review what they had learned, Dr. Washington concluded the session by negotiating a homework assignment concerning mutual self-giving and responding to each other's needs between this session and the next.

REFLECTION ON DR. WASHINGTON'S PASTORAL TEACHING

A good way to learn from Dr. Washington's illustration of pastoral teaching is to read the case story several times: once or twice out loud for an overall sense of the use of the skills, once focusing on the use of presence skills, and once concentrating on the use of the proclamation skills. When studying in a group or class, it helps to have different persons read Dr. Washington's, Wilma's, and Rich's parts.

Initial Concerns

Notice that Dr. Washington begins by exploring Rich and Wilma's initial concerns for biblical guidelines for marriage. She uses presence skills such as *accents* ("Get it right," "Ephesians thing"), *questions*, and a *summary* for this exploration. She also includes both partners by looking at Wilma questioningly to draw her out. Dr. Washington does all this in order to find out what the couple's concerns are so that she can frame her teaching to respond to them.

Expanding Their Understandings

Because expanding understandings constitutes most of the interview, it is divided into an introduction and six parts. It begins with Dr. Washington getting permission from the couple to look again at Ephesians. This is necessary because of their previous experience with this passage.

This type of concern for the couple's feelings characterizes pastoral teaching.

Introducing the passage. Notice that Dr. Washington states their feelings, supports their concerns, and addresses their issue (mutuality) in this opening section. It is important to do those three things at the beginning so that the couple stays with you.

"Be subject" parallels "love." Notice that Dr. Washington uses *sharing* to identify with the couple's question about the relationship between "be subject" and "love." She also checks constantly to see if the couple is with her, another important technique in pastoral teaching.

Dealing with feelings. Because Wilma continues to be so insistent about hearing more about the parallel between "be subject" and "love," Dr. Washington *hunches* that Wilma has been hurt by the passage. Helping people express their feelings and emotional history regarding a passage constitutes a major technique of pastoral teaching and one of the characteristics that differentiate pastoral from academic teaching. Notice how Dr. Washington supports Wilma's expression of feelings, using *informing* to challenge her unhelpful belief that she causes trouble by expressing them. This unhelpful belief and similar ones support Wilma's lack of assertiveness.

Anger. Dr. Washington continues by asking Wilma if she has more to say. After Wilma speaks, Dr. Washington identifies Wilma's anger, then uses *informing* to affirm the importance of sharing anger. It is likely that Wilma couldn't or wouldn't have shared her anger if her expression of feelings had not been supported in the previous section. Supporting her sharing of anger further challenges the unhelpful belief that anger is unchristian, a belief that supports her lack of assertiveness.

Review. Dr. Washington decides to have the couple *review* at this point in order to reinforce what Wilma has learned about the importance of expressing feelings and sharing anger. Dr. Washington wants to make sure that Wilma remembers these lessons that support assertiveness in communication and mutuality in relationships, the aims of the entire lesson. Notice that Dr. Washington uses the involvement technique of having Rich, who had been silent for a while, *review* first.

Finding out what the partners have and have not taken in constitutes a second reason for having the *review* at this point in the session. When Wilma makes her summary, Dr. Washington notices the absence of learning about the importance of anger. Thus she presses for it. Then Dr. Washington does more teaching on this point because of anger's importance for Wilma's assertiveness.

Summary of the remainder of the session. Wilma and Rich continue deepening their understanding of mutuality and its relationship to sharing feelings and needs. This is done by making the concepts concrete—identifying situations in which mutuality has or has not been done well and exploring what contributed to failure or success. Then they continue by sharing their needs for respect or nurture from each other. They do not deal with other aspects of the Ephesians passage because they are using the technique of exploring one subject deeply.

Negotiating the Contract

They contract for homework that reinforces the lessons about mutuality and sharing needs and feelings.

Summary of Reflections

The above conversation illustrates seven basic characteristics of pastoral teaching. It involves:
(1) exploring the concerns that the parishioners bring to the subject,
(2) addressing their issues as one introduces the material,
(3) inviting them to confront the pastoral resource,
(4) responding to indications of feelings and emotional history around the theme,
(5) exploring feelings and supporting their importance to learning,
(6) checking to see what the parishioners remember, and
(7) designing the rest of the session and the homework to reinforce the ideas and behaviors that challenge unhelpful beliefs and support helpful ones.

AN EXEGESIS OF EPHESIANS 5:21-33

There are five reasons for including the following extended exegesis. First, it supports Dr. Washington's interpretation of the passage. Second, it provides pastors with a different way to understand an important scriptural discussion of marriage, a point of view to which many have not been exposed. Third, this passage and the implications drawn from it considerably enrich the discussion of marriage preparation. Fourth, this exegesis provides an example of the integration of the pastor's role as biblical interpreter with the role as pastoral caregiver. Finally, this exegesis provides the biblical foundation for this book.

Ephesians 5:21-33 is the lengthiest treatment of the marital relationship in the New Testament. This passage, which is part of a "household rules" section, has been a classic text for discussing marriage throughout Christian history. For various reasons it has been used to support hierarchical marriage. Thus, conservative authors use this passage to argue against companionship marriage. Many other Christians who accept the equality of women and companionship marriage have reacted by abandoning this rich and important passage as well as other similar ones. (for example., Col. 3:18-19; Titus 2:4-5; and 1 Peter 3:1-7). Several authors (Barth 1974, Bristow 1988, Garland and Garland 1986, Jewett 1975, Scanzoni and Hardesty 1974) have read Ephesians in a different way, however; one that supports companionship marriage. The following exegesis incorporates this different way and thus mines this rich vein of Ephesians for nuggets that could enrich the contemporary practice of premarital guidance.

The Context

The key verse of the Epistle to the Ephesians is, "For he [Christ] is our peace; in his flesh he has made both groups into one and has broken down the dividing wall, that is, the hostility between us" (Eph. 2:14). All of the verses that follow must be understood in terms of the central assertion that Christ has broken down the dividing wall between opposites. The household rules section of Ephesians (5:21—6:9) applies that insight by showing how Christ has broken the dividing wall of hostility between three groups: wives and husbands, children and parents, slaves and masters. Though Paul (the author of Ephesians will be called Paul for simplicity's sake) does not eliminate all hierarchy in these relationships, he breaks down the domination that is the prime source of hostility, by making "mutual subjection (submission)" the guiding principle of these relationships. Paul sees mutual subjection as the way to repair the dividing wall of inequality between man and woman that resulted from the fall (Gen. 3:16).

The Beginning of the Passage

English readers often assume that the beginning sentence of a paragraph is the topic sentence; thus the way a passage begins is important. The discussion on marriage has traditionally begun with verse 22: "Wives, submit yourself unto your own husbands, as unto the Lord"(KJV), because the King James Version attached verse 21 to the previous paragraph. Thus readers have understood this entire passage to focus on wives' submission. Modern translations restore the proper sense of the passage by making verse 21, "Be subject to one another out of reverence for Christ," either the first sentence of the passage on marriage (21-33) or a separate sentence that provides the topic for the whole section on household rules (5:21—6:9). Putting verse 21 first tells the reader that the passage is about mutual submission between husband and wife.

The Meaning of "to Be Subject"

The Greek verb translated as "be subject" or "submit" (*hypotassomai*) is in the middle or reflexive voice, a voice that English does not have. English is limited to the active voice (the person subjects someone or something) and the passive voice (the person is subjected by someone or something). In the middle voice the subject does something that affects the subject (the husband subjects himself). Because it is in the reflexive voice, the word translated "be subject" really means "voluntarily to subject oneself."

Because *hypotassomai* is something that one voluntarily does to oneself, the English words *submit* or *subject* convey too much of a master–slave connotation to be adequate translations. Perhaps the term "self-giving" is closer to the reflexive and voluntary tone of this verb. Thus, the passage suggests mutual self-giving as the Christian guideline for marriage.

Markus Barth (1974) reminds us that the word *hypotasso* (root of *hypotassomai*) is used of military units that make themselves subordinate to other units in battle. With Ephesians 6:10-20 being a battle cry to fight the principalities and powers and fulfill the mission, the saints are compelled to support one another like soldiers: "The eschatological expectation, the need to resist enemies in the present evil day, and the missionary responsibility explain why a military term of all things received a central place in Paul's marriage counseling." (Barth 1974, 710) Thus "be subject to one another" means a mutual support of the type that sustains one another through the trials of war for the purpose of carrying out the mission.

Mutual Self-Giving

Many readers miss the mutuality of the self-giving because most English translations of verse 22 tell the wives to subject herself (self-give) to the husband. In the Greek text, however, the word for "subject" or "submit" is only in verse 21; it is not in verse 22. The Anchor Bible translation (1974) best conveys the Greek text by stating "21. Because you fear Christ subordinate yourselves to one another __ 22. ([for example]) wives to your husbands."

Thus verse 22 is not the command it appears to be in most English translations but an illustration of the overall principle of mutual submission.

Even though there is no verse that uses the term *submit yourself* in relationship to husband, verse 25 says, "Husbands, love your wives, just as Christ loved the church and gave himself up for her." There are two good reasons to believe that this instruction to "love" is parallel to "submit." First, the word for "love" in verse 25, *agape*, means the type of love that causes one to give oneself. Further, *agape* love is something done between equals (Barth 1974). Second, the image of Christ's sacrifice that follows and illustrates the command to love in verse 25 is one of self-giving: "just as Christ loved the church and *gave* himself up for her." As Bristow argues, "Both involve giving up one's self-interest to serve and care for another's. Both mean being responsive to the needs of the other. And both are commended to all Christians, as well as to husbands and wives." (Bristow 1988, 42)

If love and submission are parallel, why are different words used for husbands and wives? Perhaps Paul used different words because each gender had a different problem with self-giving and each had different needs to be met. Submission as self-giving has partly to do with issues of respect; love as self-giving has something to do with nurture and cherishing. Traditionally, men have wanted and needed respect most and women have wanted and needed nurture and romance. Yet learning to give appropriate nurture to their wives has been difficult for husbands. Likewise, those wives who have accepted their own equality have found it difficult to give respect to their husbands. Thus, Paul asks each partner to sacrifice equally by devoting him- or herself to meeting the difficult need of the other.

The clearest teaching about mutual self-giving is given in the instruction to husbands (verses 25-33). Some commentators believe that the husbands were given more instruction because what was being asked of them was more unprecedented. Others hypothesize that the writer, a man, understood men's issues better than women's. Still others speculate that Paul wanted to challenge husbands to respond to the primacy that society had given them by making the greater sacrifice. Whether for any or all of these reasons, Paul makes clear in this passage that mutual self-giving means offering up of one's life for the other as Christ did for the church. Submission for the husband means that he must take care of his wife to nourish and tenderly care for her (25-30) and that he must leave his family to create a new one (to cleave) (31). This last instruction is addressed to the husband because the bride traditionally joined his family. For him to leave his family of origin was a great sacrifice in an era in which the family was the basic economic, social, and cultural unit as well as the primary source of emotional nurture. Mutual self-giving required the husband to sacrifice himself and his relationship to his family for the purpose of nurturing his wife.

Paul's instruction to wives concerning mutual submission is much less rich than his instruction to men. He asks wives to "be subject to your husbands as you are to the Lord" (5:22) and declares that "a wife should respect her husband" (5:33). He then argues that wives should be subject because the husband is the head of the couple. Thus this part of his argument seems to be based on current societal practice. The Greek word translated "head" (kephale) was often used to mean "source." Thus Paul might be using the then-common Jewish argument that Adam had a certain position because he was the source of Eve (she was created from his rib, Gen. 2:21-22). This argument was powerful in Paul's culture, although it is not very convincing in ours. Be that as it may, some writers think that Paul was addressing a situation in which Christian wives were exercising their equality before God and their Christian liberty by leaving their marriages (Barth 1974). Paul was denying neither their equality nor their freedom; rather, he was asking wives to use their equality and freedom for their marital relationship.

Ephesians' doctrine of mutual submission is revolutionary. It makes wives' subjection voluntary in a society that required it by law and custom, and it bases this subjection primarily on reverence for Christ rather than on the culturally assumed primacy of the husband discussed in Ephesians 5:23-24. Most important, it exhorts the husband to submit to his wife (Eph. 5:25-32), a total reversal of all society's values. Surely, such a radical doctrine of Christian liberty must have been inspired by God.

Paul's doctrine of mutual submission makes more concrete the meaning of the admonition to love that begins chapter 5: "Therefore be imitators of God, as beloved children, and live in love as Christ loved us and gave himself up for us, a fragrant offering and sacrifice to God" (Eph. 5:1-2). Most importantly, mutual submission clarifies the process of becoming one flesh (Gen. 2:24), which Jesus said was God's intent for marriage (Matt. 19:4-6; Mark 10:6-9). In sum, mutual submission, or mutual self-giving, or mutual support is the process for cleaving.

Out of Reverence for Christ

Paul proposes mutual submission "out of reverence for Christ" (Eph. 5:21b). It is a response to the actions of Christ, who broke down every dividing wall by his grace (cf. Eph. 2:14). Therefore Paul recommends mutuality between husband and wife that breaks down the wall of hostility between male and female. Christ gave himself up for us (cf. Eph. 5:1-2); thus, Paul advises Christians to submit themselves to each other. Because mutual submission is a response to Christ's action, he commends it to the church, not to humanity in general. In hierarchical marriage, submission was paid to the husband as husband; in companionship marriage, it is given to the other person as person. Paul suggests going "beyond companionship" (Garland and Garland's term) and submitting to Christ, by self-giving to the other person.

In our own time, the context of mutual submission is a world in which many forces fight against marriage. "For our struggle is not against enemies of blood and flesh, but against rulers, against authorities, against the cosmic powers of this present darkness, against the spiritual forces of evil in the heavenly places" (Eph. 6:12). Contemporary writers would talk about threats to marriage in terms of: (a) the lack of support for marriage during the transition between traditional and contemporary marriage, (b) the economic, social, and cultural forces working against marriage, and (c) the fears, hurts, and sins that the partners carry from their childhoods in dysfunctional families and allow, even if unconsciously, to infect their marriages.

Resources to Sustain Mutual Submission

Paul realized that mutual submission would not be easy to do or to sustain. He knew that the devil and all the spiritual forces of evil would fight against it (Eph. 6:11b-12). Therefore he counseled the Ephesian Christians to live reflectively (Eph. 5:15-17), engage in spirit filled worship (Eph. 5:18-20), put on the armor of Christ (Eph. 6:10,13-17), and alertly and persistently intercede for the needs of others in the Christian community who are also attempting mutual submission (Eph. 6:18b). It is Christians' relationship to Christ and his church through reflection, worship, appropriation of the gospel, and intercession that enables them to imitate Christ's sacrifice by engaging in mutual submission. It is interesting to note the correlation between Paul's list of the resources that support mutual submission and Greeley's list of religious activities, found in Chapter 1, that support marriage (daily prayer, regular attendance at worship, listening to sermons that emphasize God's love, prayer retreats, and devotional reading).

Implications for Contemporary Marriage

The fifth and sixth chapters of Ephesians give helpful guidance to contemporary marriages. Three implications in particular provide the theological foundation for the emphases of communication, conflict resolution, and religious resources in this book.

(1) Mutual submission shows how to deepen the development of oneness and wholeness that partners seek in marriage. Mutual submission or mutual self-giving or mutual support is the process for cleaving. Therefore preparation for marriage can be understood as supervision of the process of mutual submission.

Such mutual support, cleaving to, or engaging each other depends on partners reordering relationships, leaving or disengaging from their families of origin. Leaving is the prerequisite for mutual support or cleaving.

(2) Mutual submission presents a vision for growth in a companionship marriage: meeting the partner's deepest need. Because mutual support asks the partners to give their lives for the rights and needs of the other, it is more radical than the modern credo by which each person struggles for his or her own rights.

In Paul's time the most difficult issue for liberated wives was giving husbands the respect and appreciation that husbands need and want; and likewise the tough issue for husbands was giving their wives the nurture and romance they needed. In our time of relatively more equality, John Gray (1992) still maintains that men have the need for respect and women the need for being cherished. The overwhelming response to his writing and workshops indicates that many people have found considerable truth to his thesis.

The process of understanding and sharing our needs requires good communication skills. Likewise, the development of suitable solutions for meeting these needs requires strong problem-solving or conflict-resolution skills.

(3) Ephesians suggests that the following activities are needed to sustain mutual submission or mutual support: worship, participation in the Christian community through intercession, appropriating the gospel, and reflection on the evil forces that would subvert the process. Thus religious resources such as rites, prayer, covenant community, and Scripture are important in marriage preparation.

Oneness through leaving family, mutual submission through communication and conflict resolution, and sustaining the willingness and ability to support through religious resources are the three implications of Ephesians 5 and 6 that undergird this book.

CONCLUSION

This chapter has used two major means of demonstrating Scripture as a pastoral resource: *first,* an illustrative conversation in which Dr. Washington used various pastoral skills and methods to challenge Wilma's anti-assertion beliefs and a reflection highlighting aspects of Dr. Washington's pastoral teaching that should be imitated. This conversation shows how Scripture can be applied to a pastoral issue. *Second,* an exegesis of Ephesians 5:21-33 provided the biblical guidelines for living and sustaining a Christian marriage. These guidelines were summarized into three implications for contemporary marriage that constitute the biblical foundation of this book: (1) leaving and cleaving as the way to marital wholeness, (2) mutual submission and the meeting of the partners' needs and the use of communication and conflict-resolution skills to do this, and (3) the importance of pastoral resources for sustaining mutual submission.

Chapter 6 presents another method of pastoral teaching, the elicitive model, in the context of preparation for the wedding service.

6

PREPARING
FOR THE WEDDING

Denominational wedding rites provide a powerful pastoral resource for couples. The rituals, readings, and prayers of these services speak directly to many of the issues and tasks that couples bring to marriage. Whether or not they choose to design their own service and use nontraditional materials, most couples interact with these official services in their minds as they plan. However, the denominational marriage services embed their wisdom in language, rituals, or concepts that many couples, often not fully churched, only partially understand. Thus, they must learn more about the meaning of the rites in order to reap their full pastoral benefits.

Having couples plan their own wedding service constitutes an effective adult method for teaching the meaning of the rite. The task of designing the wedding ceremony involves couples deeply in learning this powerful religious resource. When properly directed, and given an appropriate commentary, couples can find much in the rite that speaks to the issues and tasks with which they struggle. Thus, through planning the wedding, couples themselves apply this pastoral resource to their issues and needs. When couples plan their services, the pastor's role changes from lecturer on the meaning of the rite to facilitator in their application process.

This chapter discusses preparation for the marriage rite in five sections. In the first, Fr. Sam's conversation with Sarah and Bill illustrates an elicitive method of teaching. Next comes a section on praying the Scripture and rite. The third section presents guidance about writing a wedding policy that helps couples design their rite. Then follows a brief commentary on the wedding service to help pastors and couples relate issues, tasks, and the rite. The fifth section offers discussion of the rehearsals and family conferences.

ELICITIVE TEACHING: FR. SAM WITH SARAH AND BILL

Fr. Sam contracted for two wedding-planning sessions with Sarah and Bill, in contrast to Dr. Washington's one session with her couple. One reason for this is that the Scripture discussion forms part of wedding planning in those churches with an official liturgy, whereas the teaching of Scripture constituted a separate session for Dr. Washington. The fact that the official liturgies tend to be more elaborate and complicated is a second reason for two sessions.

Background

The first wedding-planning session was the fifth marriage-preparation session between Sarah and Bill and Fr. Sam. During the previous four, the opening session and three feedback sessions on the Prepare inventory, Fr. Sam had been impressed with this couple's openness to exploring their issues with him and with each other.

The issue of their differences came up in all of the feedback sessions. Their significant disagreements in leisure activities, financial management, spiritual beliefs, and children and parenting and the slight disagreement in personality came out on the inventory and were discussed in the feedback sessions. These disagreements were somewhat balanced by strong positive couple agreement on the other seven inventory areas. Fr. Sam, Sarah, and Bill discussed the seriousness of this level of couple disagreement, so that the couple dedicated themselves to working hard on this issue. They were assigned a problem-solving exercise at the end of the second session, and they brought a well-thought-out plan for dealing with their differences in leisure activities to the third session. They worked a lot on assertive communication and active listening in that session to deal with their differences in communication styles. In the fourth session, the couple discussed the differences between their families of origin and the various ways this had affected their relationship.

Conversation

Initial concerns. Both Bill and Sarah came to the fifth session concerned that they had not been able to complete all the parts of planning the wedding. Fr. Sam reassured them by saying that there are two wedding planning sessions because it is so hard to complete the planing in only one session.

Review of the homework. Fr. Sam then asked them what they had finished. They answered that they had read *Planning Your Marriage Service* (Weber and Weber 1992), which he had given them at the end of the fourth session. Further, they had read all the Scripture options and chosen two lessons, and they had made choices about communion, how they would process at the end of the service, who would do most of the parts of the service, and several of the prayers. Fr. Sam then affirmed them by saying, "It sounds as if you have done quite a bit of work; I hope you are proud of yourselves."

Agenda. Fr. Sam suggested the following agenda: (a) looking over the choices they had made, (b) reflecting in depth on one of the lessons, (c) looking over the choices to be made, (d) contracting assignments for next session. After asking a few questions about items b and c, and being satisfied with the pastor's rationale, Sarah and Bill agreed to the agenda.

Expanding understandings. Fr. Sam reviewed the choices that they had made, checking to see that they had agreed on them and if they had a rationale for each. When he was satisfied, he asked, "Which of the lessons really struck you?" Sarah immediately answered, "The long one on love." Bill, pondered a moment and then agreed: "The reading from First Corinthians was the most powerful for me, also."

"What struck you about this reading?" the pastor asked, looking at them both. Sarah replied, "It's just so beautiful, so beautiful. Everyone thinks so; all my friends chose that one for their weddings." "What's so beautiful for you, Sarah?" queried Fr. Sam. "Well, I don't know, it's just the way it talks about such a deep kind of love, such a wonderful love." "And you, Bill?" the pastor probed. "Well, I don't want to overstate the case, Father, but that passage describes the way that I have felt since I've known Sarah: a lot more loving." "More loving?" queried Fr. Sam. "Yes, I'm more open about people and things—even my buddies at work have noticed it."

"So the passage applies to you, Bill, in that it talks about how being with Sarah has made you act. Sarah, how has it applied to you?" "Well, it is the kind of love that I dream of and pray that I can give Bill," Sarah responded. Fr. Sam commented, "It sounds as if the passage has great meaning for both of you. Bill hears it as talking about what has begun to happen to him, and Sarah wants to have this kind of love. Is that about right?" "Yes," answered Sarah, "and I guess I have a little bit of that kind of love, too."

Then Fr. Sam asked, "How did you two deal with the idea in the commentary [Weber and Weber 1992, 33] that this passage is not about human love but God's love?" After a pause, Sarah responded, "I knew so deep a love was God's love; that's why I have prayed for God to share it through me, so that Bill and I might experience more of it." There was another long pause and Bill spoke: "I . . . didn't know quite what to make of it . . . being about God's love . . . so I applied it to my experience to make sense of it." Fr. Sam smiled and said, "It is difficult to grasp, isn't it? Why don't you take a moment to read the commentary and passage over again and see what comes to you?"

During the silence while Bill was reading, the pastor prayed for Bill's heart to be opened. When Bill had finished, he declared, "Well, I guess the love I have been feeling is from God . . . the book says that it is an experience of God. But I have never thought about our romance or about God in that way." "Why don't you take some time right now and think about it that way," Fr. Sam suggested quietly, "and see what happens."

Both Sarah and Bill became silently pensive for a while, and the pastor continued to pray in his heart. Then Bill remarked, "It feels strange to think of God in terms of feeling love. I have always connected him with rules and duty—you know, what you can do and what you can't or shouldn't do. The only feelings I connected with God were fear and guilt." "Strange to think of God in terms of love," reflected Fr. Sam. "Yes," Bill responded. "It makes what Sarah and I feel for each other sort of . . . holy, or something like that. It just . . . turns everything around, doesn't it?"

After considerably more discussion about the implications of God being love, and love being the experience of God, Fr. Sam asked Sarah and Bill another question: "How does all this relate to the issue of your differences that we have spent so much time talking about during the last four sessions?" The room became quiet again as the couple mulled over this question. Then Sarah blurted out, "You need the kind of love that 'endures all things' to get along in the midst of a lot of differences." "Yes, Sarah," Bill agreed, "It's the differences between us that sometimes bring out impatience and jealousy and that sort of thing in me. It's these differences that require this Godly love." The three of them spent a few more minutes exploring this insight.

Then the pastor asked, "So what have you already done with these differences to increase your love?" Again there was a long pause before Bill answered: "Well, it seems to me that we tried to work out the differences as a way of building our love, like we did with the leisure activities plan." Fr. Sam responded, "That's a good answer, but what happens with those differences that don't respond to a plan?" "Those are the ones that drove me to pray for enough love to endure," Sarah interjected. "Two good answers: Work out differences to build your love, and pray for love to endure the differences that remain." "It sounds like you have used two good strategies to act out the meaning of this passage," summarized Fr. Sam.

"How do you want to implement these understandings this week?" was the pastor's next query. "We could do another plan like the leisure activities plan," responded Bill. "That has been successful." "That's a good idea, Bill," Sarah said, "but I wonder if we ought to try something new, like praying together about our differences?" "Those are two very good answers," said Fr. Sam. "Which do you choose?" "I'm not to sure how to do the prayer thing," confessed Bill. "That's why I think we ought to do it, honey," Sarah replied. "Well, Fr. Sam, if we were to try the prayer thing, what would we do?" asked Bill. Fr. Sam answered, "Let me show you a method of praying that might be helpful." (See "Praying the Rite and Scripture," page 89.)

Negotiate the contract. After going over the parts of the service that they had not planned, they were ready to work out the homework for the next session. The first assignment was to finish planning the service. The second was to use the method of praying the First Corinthians passage (see page 89) that Fr. Sam had shown them daily until the next session.

The Six Questions

Elicitive teaching involves drawing wisdom out of couples. This is done by asking them reflective questions about the choices that they have made. Thus couples are active in making the connections rather than passive as the pastor makes the connections. The six particularly important questions for elicitive teaching are: (1) How did you choose these lessons, or prayers, or rituals? (2) Which portion would you like to discuss? (3) What does it mean to you? (4) How does it relate to the issues with which you have been dealing? (5) How have you acted its meaning out? (6) How could you act this out this week?

(1) How did you choose these lessons, or prayers, or rituals? This basic question aims to determine whether or not the couple worked together in making choices. If not, there may be communication, conflict-resolution, or involvement issues that need to be addressed. This question is important, because there must be a foundation of joint ownership of the decision to choose the particular lesson, prayer, or ritual for the other five questions to be effective. For example, Fr. Sam determined that Sarah and Bill had worked together on choosing during the Reviewing of Preparation above.

(2) Which portion would you like to discuss? This question gives the couple the choice of the particular lesson, prayer, or ritual to be discussed. Their choice is important for several reasons. First, it gives them more stake in the discussion. Second, the portion with the most attraction for them usually attracts them for a purpose. It has some wisdom that they need to uncover. Near the beginning of "Expanding Understandings," Fr. Sam used a variation of this second question: "What lesson particularly struck you?"

(3) What does it mean to you? The question seeks to determine how each partner understands the portion of the rite that they have chosen to discuss. Their understandings must be unearthed so that the pastor can know what needs to be affirmed and what needs to be expanded. In the conversation summarized above, Fr. Sam asked this third question in the following form: "What struck you about this lesson?" He found out that Bill saw it as describing his growing love and Sarah saw it as the deep love to which she aspired.

Neither talked about the love as God's love, so Fr. Sam used a form of the skill of *contending* to challenge their understandings. He asked them how they dealt with the commentary's understanding of the passage as talking about God's love rather than human love. This sent them back to wrestle with the commentary again until their understandings were expanded.

This third question constitutes the center or fulcrum of the elicitive teaching process; it unearths the couples' understandings that need to be challenged or affirmed. The first two questions lay the foundation of interest in the passage that sustains the third question. Questions four, five, and six apply the expanded understanding developed in response to the third question.

(4) How does it relate to the issues with which you have been dealing? This question asks for conceptual application of the expanded understanding. Conceptual application is the first step in the application process. Fr. Sam asked the conceptual application question in the following manner: "How does all this relate to the issue of your differences that we have spent so much time talking about during the last four sessions?"

(5) How have you acted its meaning out? This question asks the couple to apply their conceptual understanding behaviorally. They must take two steps: First, decide what the expanded understanding looks like in real life; second, recall when they have already applied the expanded understanding. The first step helps make the expanded understanding more concrete; it moves it from a concept to a set of behaviors. The second step directs them to find a set of behaviors on which they can build. According to behavior modification theory, it is more effective to increase a behavior that has already been done than to try to teach a new one. Fr. Sam used this form of question five above: "So what have you already done with these differences to increase your love?"

(6) How could you act this out this week? The final question points to the future; how do you intend to act out what you have learned? Planning to do specific behaviors in response to one's expanded understanding constitutes the final pre-action level of making the understanding concrete.

"How do you want to implement these understandings this week?" was Fr. Sam's version of the query.

Along with these questions, pastors need to use the presence skills to explore the partners' answers. Likewise, after due exploration, pastors use proclamation skills to affirm or dispute their answers.

Action constitutes the goal of this particular elicitive teaching method. The words of James echo in this process "be doers of the word, and not merely hearers . . . [be] . . . not hearers who forget but doers who act" (James 1:22, 25).

PRAYING THE RITE AND SCRIPTURE

After Fr. Sam said, "Let me show you a method of praying that might be helpful," he gave each of them a copy of the handout "Praying the Service and Scriptures." Then he asked them to take a couple of minutes to look over the first two paragraphs and the section on "Praying as a couple." (See Appendix B.)

When they had finished reviewing the program and looked up, the pastor asked them if there were any questions. Bill asked if they had to keep reading the commentary each day, and Fr. Sam *revised* the program by saying that they had worked on it enough today so that they did not have to keep repeating it. Since there were no more questions, the pastor invited them to *rehearse* the procedure right then. After about fifteen minutes of practice, Fr. Sam praised them for how well they had done. Then Sarah and Bill discussed with him what had come to them in prayer. Bill had experienced a warm feeling with no words and wondered if that was enough. Sarah had sensed that she was somewhat jealous of Bill's ability to be alone. After assuring them that these results were fine and that more would come to them during the week as they continued to pray about this passage, Fr. Sam concluded the session.

ELEMENTS OF A MARRIAGE POLICY

Pastors must provide a written policy that states the boundaries within which couples must work as they design the service and attendant ceremonies. For instance, may they throw rice? Who advises them on decorations? A written framework allows couples to do much of the planning on their own, instead of constantly having to check with the pastor as if they were dependent children.

The wedding or marriage policy of the congregation provides support for both the pastor and the couple. It supports couples by giving them the information they need to make an informed choice about participating in the congregation's wedding process. It also gives couples the benefit of the congregation's, the denomination's, and the faith tradition's wisdom about weddings and marriage. Finally, the policy helps couples by requiring those activities that will give them a good opportunity to experience a religious wedding.

The policy also supports pastors, first, by protecting them from demands to perform services that contradict their beliefs or from working with couples who do not intend to explore religious marriage preparation. Fr. Sam would not have had to be so concerned about Sarah and Bill's intentions if St. Paul's had had a wedding policy that raised this issue. Further, the policy gives pastors the assurance of the congregation's support for the marriage-preparation ministry. If Fr. Sam had had a wedding policy that had been adopted by the key congregational structures, he would have been immune from any political fallout had he refused to marry Bill and Sarah because of their noncompliance with the policy.

I designed the following outline after reading many congregational marriage policies:

1. Welcoming preamble
2. Statement on the denominational meaning of marriage
3. Statement of congregational policies
   - Qualifications for marriage in this congregation and in this state
   - Minimum advance notice needed to schedule wedding
   - Marriage preparation (length, cost, by whom)
   - When date may be set (e.g., after conference with clergy)
   - Wedding coordinator (e.g., when and how to contact)
   - Limitations to use of properties (e.g., no rice, policies on alcohol use)
   - On planning the wedding service
   - On musicians
   - On rehearsals
   - On photographers, videographers, and picture taking
   - On flowers and decorations

4. Charges and fees (*A* for pledging members; *B* for others)

	A	*B*
Use of the church (main sanctuary)	*A*	*B*
Janitorial services	*A*	*B*
Organist	*A*	*B*
Wedding coordinator (Altar Guild)	*A*	*B*
Total Cost		
Use of rooms for reception	*A*	*B*
Janitorial services	*A*	*B*
Reception coordinator	*A*	*B*
Total Cost		

   - When payment is due
   - To whom which checks are written

5. Closing statement (reiterating the welcome; naming the person to whom to address questions about the document)

Lyle E. Schaller (1988), one of the nation's top church consultants, recommends changing the wedding policy as one key way to increase church attendance. Churches should change from a policy that charges nonmembers for the use of the building to one that invites nonmembers to worship with you. Schaller recommends a policy such as that of a parish in Texas:

> The only requirements for being married here now are (a) the minister must be willing to perform the wedding for that particular couple, (b) one or both parties must have attended worship here for at least six Sundays in the three months before the wedding is scheduled, or (c) one or both parties must be from a family who are members. (65–66)

This parish found that this policy produced "at least two dozen members who are regular attenders" in the last five years. I have heard of similar positive church growth results in congregations that require significant church attendance as part of the qualification for marriage. Conversely, there are few reports of significant numbers of couples becoming part of the congregation in which they were married when church attendance is not required.

I include the following stipulation in the qualifications for marriage for situations in which one partner practices the faith and the other does not:

> The pastor will do the wedding if the non-practicing partner has: (1) an open mind willing to explore and discuss the religious issues about marriage that the wedding service raises, (2) a willingness to experiment with the religious practices that support marriage and are assumed by the wedding service, and (3) a commitment to support the practicing partner in her or his religious practice after the wedding.

The non-practicing partner's willingness to experiment with religious practices would include attending Sunday worship.

A mentor program in which the engaged couple meets with a mentor couple for several scheduled sessions of informal conversation can help a couple integrate into the congregation. For example, Sarah and Bill's mentor couple shared with them the importance of Sunday worship to their own married lives. Then they invited them personally to come to church several times. When Sarah and Bill arrived at St. Paul's, they sat with their mentor couple, who helped Sarah follow the service and afterwards introduced the couple to other couples their age during the coffee hour.

A written marriage policy gives couples a handy guide to the regulations for having their wedding in a particular congregation's church building or solemnized by its clergy. The policy offers such information as who is qualified to be married, what the marriage preparation program is, how the building may be used, whom you consult about flowers and decorations, and the cost. It is important that the policy be written so that the couple can refer to it on their own. In addition, a written policy lets them know that the rules apply to all and were not made up just to frustrate them. If this policy is to be enforced, it must be reviewed and accepted by the appropriate leadership of the congregation.

A PASTOR'S BRIEF COMMENTARY ON THE RITE

When possible, pastors should provide or recommend a brief written commentary on the service and on each of the suggested Scripture readings. This document should include the specifics of planning the marriage rite, thus providing the couple with the information they need to make wise and relevant choices. Such commentaries make teaching the service in sessions easier because much of the instruction happens before the meeting. Pastors may use the following brief commentary in constructing their own commentaries on the wedding rite that they use: This brief ecumenical commentary reflects the Catholic, Episcopal, Lutheran, Methodist, Presbyterian, and United Church of Christ marriage services without communion.[3] It considers the Wedding Rite as a three-act drama with each act devoted to one of the three tasks of marrying: leaving, getting a blessing, and cleaving. Each act has ritual actions and content that express deep wisdom about its particular task. All of the services considered allow couples to choose some of the rituals and content of each act. This commentary describes each act and suggests some of the couple needs and tasks it addresses.

Act One: Leaving

Act one, the first and longest act, expresses the theme of leaving. As stated in Chapter 4, leaving means that each partner reorders relationships with family and friends in order to enter into the new central relationship of marriage. This act has two foci: acting out the intention to leave and accepting the gift of the church's wisdom about marriage to take on the journey.

The intention to leave. The services act out the couple's intention to leave in three ways: first, in the manner that the bride, groom, witnesses, and pastor get in place before the congregation; second, in the couple's declaration or indication of the intention to marry; and third, by the family and congregational rituals of support for their leaving.

(1) Getting in place. How the wedding party assumes their places constitutes the first major choice in act one. In the traditional entrance rite, the groom and clergy entered from the side and waited for the bride, who processed up the aisle on the arm of her father. This ritual acts out a former legal situation in which one owner, the father, gave his property, the bride, to a new owner, the groom. Since that legal situation no longer exists in North America, how then does the wedding party assume their places?

The couple must decide how the reordering of relationships will be acted out in the process of getting in place. Is the bride to be the star of the wedding, marching in solitary splendor? How should parents, children, and friends be included in the entrance? In Wilma's situation (Chapter 4), her confusion about leaving tempted her to require her daughters to be a part of the wedding party so that it would be theirs also. After conversation with Dr. Washington, she expressed this reordering of relationships by not requiring her daughters to be part of the procession.

(2) Declaration of intention. Reflection on the apparent redundancy of the declaration of intention and the wedding vows in one service can be helpful for the partners. Whether they are denying the sadness or finality of leaving or are openly wrestling with the question of committing, all partners have difficulty with leaving.

(3) Rituals of affirmation. The ritual of family affirmation or family and congregational affirmation of the couple's intention serves as a reminder of the importance of support from family, friends, and church in sustaining a marriage. This ritual of family affirmation is the more inclusive successor to the ritual of the father giving the bride, now only found as an option in the Episcopal service. This affirmation constitutes the third ritual of reordering the relationships between partner(s) and family.

Those couples using the Episcopal service must choose whether to have a giving or presentation ritual, and, if so, how it should be done. Thus, the couple must ask what family and personal needs such a ceremony would address or confuse. For example, Sarah wanted to honor her mother, so she suggested that they each have both parents present them. Bill, who had been trying to think of a way to involve his father, agreed with her.

The church's wisdom. All of the nuptial rites considered share the wisdom of the church about marriage in four ways: a statement about marriage, the texts of the music used, the recommended Scripture readings, and the sermon. In most rites, the couples have three major choices about the presentation of the church's wisdom. The first concerns the texts of the hymns, musical presentations, psalm, or anthems used in the service. The second involves choice of readings. The services considered all had suggestions for appropriate Scripture readings. Third, in all but the Catholic and Methodist liturgies, which require a witness, the couple must decide whether or not to have a sermon.

(1) Statement on marriage. The statement on Christian marriage found in each of the rites gives solid teaching about marriage that can be helpful in correcting the secular and romantic marriage expectations and understandings of many couples.

(2) Musical texts. Christian hymn texts, anthems based on Scripture, and metrical psalms have much to teach about the meaning of love, God's grace, and Christian marriage. The process of considering and choosing these, instead of popular songs that praise romantic love and secular values, can be a major source of education for the couple.

(3) Readings and sermon. The readings and the sermon can help the couple deal with a particular issue unique to their relationship or it can help them and the congregation contrast the scriptural and church's understanding of marriage with secular and romantic notions. For instance, Fr. Sam used First Corinthians as a text, and the conversations he had with Sarah and Bill on this passage to focus on how differences can deepen love. His sermon invited the couple and those assembled to leave the safety of their differences and to walk through the waters of conflict and problem solving until they cross over into a new land of love and liberty.

Act Two: Getting a Blessing

Act two addresses the central task of the wedding: getting a blessing. As stated in Chapter 4, the word *blessing* has many different meanings woven together in it. It means "dedication," for to bless something is to set it apart. Another meaning is "to sanctify, to make holy." A related meaning is "to protect;" those things that are made holy are understood as protected by God. Act two has three parts, all of which have to do with blessing: vows, exchanging symbols, and the declaration of marriage.

The vows. The vows act out blessing as dedication and setting apart. In these the partners commit themselves exclusively to each other until parted by death. In some services, couples may only choose between sets of vows in the worship book; in others, they may choose between the written options and writing their own vows. In a few denominations, only the given set of vows may be used. In any of these cases, a discussion of the meaning of the vows will help educate the couple about the Christian understanding of marriage and set that understanding apart from secular and romantic perceptions.

Exchanging symbols (rings). After the pronouncing of the vows comes the time to exchange symbols of permanent commitment, usually a ring or rings. An important question that may focus a couple's understanding of marriage is, Do you intend to have a single- or double-ring ceremony, and why?

Declaration of the marriage. This declaration expresses blessing as approval. It announces God's and the church's approval, and, when done according to the laws of the state, the state's approval and protection also. The couple marries each other by saying the vows. This declaration invites the protection and respect of these vows by all others.

Act Three: Cleaving

Act three begins the continuing process of sustaining the couple in their vows. It does this by including prayers of intercession or thanksgiving for the couple, a blessing by the minister, the peace (bride and groom's kiss), and a procession out. Act three teaches that sustaining the couple involves prayer by the couple and the church and physical intimacy between the partners.

Prayers of intercession or thanksgiving. The intercessions and thanksgivings written for this act contain much wisdom about what sustains a marriage. In most services, choices must be made, and therefore couples must consider the teachings of these prayers. These prayers are by or on behalf of the congregation; therefore they instruct the congregation, family, and friends in what they ought to pray for to support this marriage.

Blessing by the minister. All of the services considered have a special clerical blessing of the newly married couple. This blessing, especially when done in the context of a helpful and healthy relationship with the minister, or the minister's deputy for premarital guidance, gives the couple the assurance they need to begin the process of cleaving.

The peace. The traditional kiss of the bride and groom echo the Kiss of Peace, a part of ancient liturgies that has returned to many modern services. This kiss as the couple's climactic ritual in the third act of the service teaches two important truths: first, that Christianity is not anti-sex or anti-flesh; second, that physical intimacy has a central place in cleaving, or building and sustaining the marriage.

The procession out. The final choices in planning the wedding have to do with how the wedding party recesses. Decisions must be made: Who goes out in the procession, and who leaves in another way? Is there music, and, if so, what music?

REHEARSAL AND FAMILY CONFERENCE

I have found two other very helpful ways to prepare for weddings: rehearsals and family conferences. Each of these help the couple and other participants to involve themselves more fully in both the wedding and the marriage process.

The Rehearsal

The rehearsal has two purposes. The first and most obvious is to prepare the wedding party for their leadership in the wedding service. Because the family, witnesses, and other members of the party are "onstage," their demeanor and participation during the rite has a great effect on the congregation and the bride and groom. Thus the wedding party needs to know their parts well enough to do them comfortably. Going though the service once verbally and walking through the ceremony twice, the second time in an abbreviated manner, generally proves to be sufficient.

Because part of this group's leadership involves making the congregational verbal responses clearly and forcefully, these should be rehearsed. Finally, special efforts should be made to help the unchurched or those who are no longer churched feel comfortable.

Educating the couple, their families, and friends about marriage and their role in it constitutes the second and more important purpose for the rehearsal. Therefore, the rehearsal leader should discuss the meaning of each part of the ceremony, particularly highlighting those parts which counteract secular and romantic notions. The wedding party should be thoroughly instructed in the implications of their promises to support the couple in marriage. Such training should include discussion of several common couple situations and the proper response or responses for family and friends.

In order for rehearsals to fulfill their purposes, three conditions must be met. First, all members of the wedding party should be there on time and sober. Second, the wedding should be thoroughly planned before the rehearsal. Third, the rehearsal should be conducted in a quiet and prayerful manner.

I have found it helpful to have other members of the congregation with special responsibilities for weddings present at the rehearsal. Members of the Altar Guild or Wedding Coordinators Committee can support the prayerful mood, help arrange processions, direct participants, and answer questions about flowers, runners, and so forth. The couple's mentors can give the couple and other participants support and help interpret and apply the actions and words of the wedding rite.

The Family Conference

The family conference brings together the couple and each of their parents to prepare for the marriage. When the parents have been divorced and remarried, the couple invites the spouses also. This session allows the parents to pass on their verbal wisdom about marriage together. It accentuates the leaving process by inviting the parents to give their last words to their children, before they become married. The family conference usually happens a day or two before the wedding, thus helping the couple, parents, and pastor to become bonded before the rehearsal and nuptials. I have found that even poorly functioning parents have made helpful contributions by acknowledging their issues and suggesting how they got caught up in them. I can imagine situations in which the parents are so dysfunctional and completely without insight that a family conference should not be held. It is likely that the child of such parents and his or her partner would need couples therapy in addition to premarital guidance because their familial relationship training had been so impoverished.

The couple sets up the family conference by inviting parents (and stepparents) at the beginning of the premarital guidance process to share their wisdom with them at this special time in their lives. When the families arrive, the pastor reminds them that: (a) They have been their children's teacher about marriage, mostly by what they have done; (b) most parents have had problems adjusting at the beginning of marriage; (c) this is the last time to give advice to their child as a single person; in the future they must respect their marriage. Then the pastor tells the parents (and stepparents) that each will be given a chance to talk, while the engaged couple takes notes. Next the pastor asks each of the parents (and stepparents) to give one bit of advice about how to succeed in marriage. The pastor draws persons out and keeps the conversation moving when necessary. When the parents (and stepparents) have finished, the pastor summarizes their insights as a way of concluding the session.

The family conference described above has been adapted by this author from the one proposed by Stahmann and Hiebert in *Premarital Counseling* (1987, 102–4). I have found the family conference to be a very helpful part of premarital guidance: (a) It prepares the parents (and stepparents) to relate to their children as a married couple; (b) it gives the parents (and stepparents) a chance to share their wisdom; (c) it gives the partners new respect for their divorced parents' ability to be constructive with each other; (d) it brings each partner closer to his or her future in-laws; (e) it helps the parents to establish a relationship to the pastor and vice versa; (f) it helps the parents, partners, and pastor to be more at ease with one another during the rehearsal and ceremony. Yet providing a helpful way to negotiate the partners' leaving of the family of origin remains the most important function of this meeting. It helps the partners to disengage with their families so that they can engage with each other.

CONCLUSION

This chapter has completed the two-chapter section on applying pastoral resources to couple needs and tasks. It has presented an elicitive method of teaching. This method and the pastoral teaching method introduced in Chapter 5 both can be used to teach Scripture or the wedding rite. A method for praying Scripture and the rite was discussed to help couples prepare prayerfully for their nuptials. This was followed by an outline for constructing a congregational wedding policy that would give couples information and guidance in wedding planning. Then a brief commentary was provided to help pastors understand the pastoral teaching potential of the rite, as well as to give them aid in developing their own commentaries for couples. This chapter concluded with brief presentations about the wedding rehearsal and the family conference, two other ways for couples and their families (and friends) to prepare for the wedding.

7

REFLECTIONS

The book has presented a new model of premarital counseling called "Premarital Guidance." This construct integrates helping skills with secular and religious resources to provide religious marriage preparation for couples. Unlike some other methods of premarital counseling, premarital guidance affirms pastors' multiple roles as preacher and teacher, worship leader, evangelist, administrator, spiritual guide, and facilitator of ministries.

Two pastors, Fr. Sam and Dr. Washington, encountered the premarital guidance model in a workshop. This book has presented the method, concepts, and resources that they studied in the workshop, as well as their experiences in using this model. It concludes with their reflections on how this material and their use of the model responded to the questions that they brought to the workshop.

Dr. Washington: When I took the position as Minister for Families at Greater Mount Zion (GMZ) a year ago, I realized that I hadn't been trained in premarital counseling, yet premarital work would be a significant part of my ministry. So I looked around for some continuing education in this area and there wasn't much. I did find this five-day workshop on something called "Premarital Guidance," so I attended it.

I brought lots of questions to this workshop. There were the standard questions: What is the church's ministry to engaged couples? Which couples should we take on? What are our goals? What materials and resources can we use? As a trained pastoral counselor I had other questions such as: How do I use my counseling skills in a way that witnesses to the gospel? How can I use Scripture and prayer to help this couple? Now that I am a local church pastor, should I refer this couple even though I would have counseled them as a psychotherapist?

Fr. Sam: I brought the same standard questions as you did, Claretta, but my other concerns were different. I wondered if premarital counseling really worked. Honestly, I was frustrated with this ministry because I couldn't see many results. Not many of the couples I worked with joined this or any other church. I had a hard time getting into in-depth discussions about marriage with couples who only seemed interested in a wedding. I was at a loss for ways to bring to the surface the most strategic issues for discussion. And like everyone else I wanted to know how to turn marriage-preparation time into more than an obligation.

Dr. Washington: Let's look at the standard questions first, OK? The workshop certainly addressed them. The leaders talked about premarital guidance as one part of the congregation's life-long ministry. They stressed two implications of that statement: (a) Pastors didn't have to teach couples everything during marriage preparation; (b) pastors should try to integrate couples into the congregation. That point led to the next, that pastors should prepare only those couples who were interested in religious marriage preparation, those who would be likely candidates for church participation.

Fr. Sam: That point was a real eye-opener for me. Perhaps the reason that so few couples I worked with joined the church was that I didn't restrict preparation to those who showed some willingness to do so. I also found some of the suggestions for integrating engaged couples into the congregation interesting, such as the mentoring couples program, the requirement that couples attend church before being married in church, and involving couples in classes on marriage with other engaged and married couples from the congregation. I tried the mentoring program and the mentor couple did wonders in getting Sarah and Bill active in the congregation.

Dr. Washington: I tried the other two strategies. I had Wilma and Rich attend a marriage class that met right before the main service. And it worked—they became more involved in the congregation. But they weren't a tough case, because they were already coming to church. But another couple, Oprah and Fred, who weren't coming to church, started coming regularly as a result of the class.

But getting back to the standard questions, the leaders presented an interesting set of the goals for premarital guidance. Remember them, Sam?

Fr. Sam: You bet I remember one, because I had a lot of difficulty with the first goal: religious marriage preparation, education in the beliefs and practices in a religious wedding service. It wasn't until they talked about the research that showed the importance of religiosity for longevity and happiness in marriage that I thought seriously about this as a goal. I had always asked, "Why I should teach religious understandings to them during marriage preparation? Isn't dealing with the practicalities of marriage difficult enough?"

Another goal, I believe, was to help couples with their tasks of leaving, getting a blessing, and cleaving. The workshop emphasized the decision as to whether or not to marry a couple on the basis of their readiness and willingness to engage these tasks. Claretta, those were the only two goals I can remember; were there others?

Dr. Washington: A third goal had to do with developing communication and conflict-resolution skills. Remember how they talked about these being the foundational skills for building a companionship marriage? A fourth goal was for the couples to consider the eleven topics that are important for marriage preparation.

Fr. Sam: You mean the ones that were covered by the Prepare inventory? Well, while we are talking about that inventory, I am certainly impressed with it, because it raised the important issues for Sarah and Bill to talk about. It really answered my questions about how to get couples to talk about real problems and marriage, not just mumble platitudes and focus on the wedding. And the research they presented showed me that premarital guidance can work.

Dr. Washington: I also found Prepare to be a tremendous resource for structuring a couple's class. It got the partners really talking to each other about things that mattered. And Prepare even helped me to understand how Wilma was a part of her problem with Henry, her ex-husband, by identifying her nonassertive communication style.

While we are talking about resources, let me say that as a trained counselor I found some of the workshop redundant, such as how to structure the sessions and how to listen.

But, I did find two resources very helpful, the metanoia model and the characteristics of pastoral teaching. The metanoia model really showed me a way to use my counseling skills to witness to the gospel by combining helping skills, proclaiming skills, and the use of religious resources. Likewise the characteristics of pastoral teaching showed me how to use my counseling skills in teaching Scripture. I tried this with Wilma and Rich and it really worked.

Fr. Sam: Since I haven't had the training that you have, I was really helped by the training in helping skills and the constructing of sessions. Yet I didn't fully understand the whole metanoia model. Anyway, I used the six questions for elicitive teaching and the instruction sheet on Praying Service and Scriptures with Sarah and Bill. I was really pleased with the results. These resources allowed me to teach religion to a nonpracticing couple in a way that invited them to practice. Also, we are working on a wedding policy right now based on the outline that was presented. And the Pastor's Brief Commentary on the Rite was a helpful background resource when I went over the service with the couple, though I found a longer, more detailed Episcopal commentary even more helpful (Weber and Weber 1992).

Another important resource was the suggestion of an introductory session, three feedback sessions, two sessions for planning the wedding service, and a wedding rehearsal. It seemed a lot at first, but all of our sessions were well-used, and I really think we got somewhere. Spending six sessions and a wedding rehearsal with a couple doesn't seem to be a waste of time, if you work only with couples that are likely candidates for active church membership. What do you think, Claretta?

Dr. Washington: I agree. In fact, I expanded the model by enrolling Wilma and Rich in a class and then having five sessions with them. The five sessions were two individual and one joint session on their divorces, and a Scripture session and a wedding planning session. Actually we have done only four of these sessions so far because it became clear to all three of us that they were not ready to get married yet. Both were too emotionally entangled with their ex-spouses and needed some time and work to be free, so they postponed the wedding. I think that the resources I used, such as Prepare and the class combined with the time for premarital guidance that I demanded, gave them an opportunity to see that they weren't ready yet.

But all that time has not been wasted for either them or me. They are enjoying themselves better as a couple because of all of that training in communication and conflict-resolution skills, family-of-origin exploration, and digesting a scriptural understanding of marriage. It became clear to me, because of the multiple contacts that we had with my meeting them individually and in class and in church, that I couldn't keep the necessary therapeutic distance from this couple. Therefore I took this opportunity to practice dealing with the couple as a pastor and not as a counselor. It's been a learning experience to refer them and support them rather than be their therapist.

You know, Sam, I have shared the responses to all of my questions about the four standard questions. What about you?

Fr. Sam: I only want to say that I'm a lot more hopeful about premarital guidance than I was before the workshop and the work it inspired with Sarah and Bill.

Dr. Washington: Amen, brother, Amen.

If you would like to contact the author to give feedback or to find out more about his seminars, please send him an e-mail at charleswt@aol.com.

APPENDIX A

WORKBOOKS

Workbooks provide information and exercises for the couple to use alone and thus help them to learn experientially. One of their strengths is the solid information they provide on most of the topics. Another is their emphasis on the importance of the couple's participation in their marriage preparation.

Two solid workbooks are Grenz and Glover's (1996) *The Marriage Journey* and Hunt and Hunt's (1982) *Preparing for Christian Marriage.* The latter addresses family and friends, personality, expectations, communication, conflict resolution, sexuality, money, children, leisure (recreation and community), church and spirituality, and the wedding in eleven short but helpful chapters, each with several exercises and questions for couple discussion. *The Marriage Journey* can be used for marriage preparation, marriage enrichment, and training of marriage mentors. In ten information-packed chapters it discusses the Theology of Marriage, Family and Friends, Marital Expectations, Conflict Resolution, Finances, Sexuality, Children, Marriage Preparation, and the Journey Ahead. There are numerous discussion questions for engaged couples and one or two projects in each chapter. This book is more informational, theological, and didactic than the Hunts' book.

Many pastors would choose the Hunts' book because of the quality of its interactive exercises. Other pastors would choose Grenz and Glover because of the richness of its thinking written in a popular idiom. Episcopal pastors would particular enjoy Grenz and Glover's exposition of quotes from the *Book of Common Prayer* wedding service.

These workbooks have several weaknesses when used alone. First, the absence of a third person means that there is no one to observe and coach the couple's communication and conflict resolution. Second, this lack of a third person robs the couple of an objective party to help them discuss difficult issues more comfortably and insightfully. Finally, workbooks assume that the quality of information, not the depth of communication and the positive couple agreement, provides the best basis for a successful marriage, whereas the research (Druckman et al. 1979; Flowers and Olson 1986; Hawley and Olson 1995; Larsen and Olson 1989; Olthoff 1989) indicates that the depth of communication and positive couple agreement correlate strongly with happy marriages. These workbooks work best with the minority of people who learn primarily through reading. Because of their weaknesses when used by themselves, I do not recommend them as the sole resource for premarital guidance. Workbooks can be very helpful when combined with inventories or as part of courses.

PREMARITAL INVENTORIES

Premarital inventories are questionnaires that focus on the partners' knowledge of and opinions about the standard topics discussed in marriage preparation. They differ from personality tests in that premarital inventories measure the presence or absence of positive couple agreement on the topics, whereas personality tests focus on the individual's feelings and individual personality issues.

Three widely used premarital inventories are Markey, Micheletto, and Becker's (1997) *Facilitating Open Couple Communication, Understanding and Study* (FOCCUS); Velander's (1993) *The Premarriage Awareness Inventory* (PAI); and Olson's (1996) *Prepare/Enrich Inventory* (P/E). All three of these inventories cover the essential topics for premarital preparation. The creators of each of these inventories envision its results being discussed in feedback sessions with engaged couples. PAI and P/E have accompanying workbooks for the couples.

Facilitating Open Couple Communication, Understanding and Study

The 189-statement FOCCUS inventory is four inventories in one: a basic inventory, all couples respond to statements 1–156; Interchurch couples also respond to statements 157–64; if one or both partners are entering a second marriage, both partners respond to statements 165–73; and if the couple is cohabiting, they also respond to statements 174–89. The basic 156 statements cover twelve content areas: Life-Style Expectations, Friends and Interests, Personality Match, Personal Issues, Communication, Problem-Solving, Religion and Values, Parenting Issues, Extended Family Issues, Sexuality Issues, Financial Issues, Readiness Issues, and Marriage Covenant. In addition to the twelve content areas, three summary categories are drawn from the couple's responses to the 156 statements: Key Problem Indicators, Family of Origin Statements, Dual Career Statements. There are also three special content areas: Interfaith Marriages (statements 157–64), Second Marriages (statements 165–73), and Cohabiting Couples (statements 174–89). Responses to Domestic Violence statements are also summarized.

This program comes in three editions: Roman Catholic, Christian Nondenominational, and Non-denominational. The same statements in modified wording appear in all three editions. There are workbooks in Spanish and statement booklets in Alternate English (learning disabled), Spanish, Vietnamese, Italian, and Polish.

The FOCCUS packet contains a Facilitator Manual that introduces the inventory, describes its administration and scoring, provides guidelines for interpretation of the inventory, and presents a process for facilitating couple discussion of the inventory results. The packet also contains FOCCUS answer sheets suitable for computer scoring, and a pair of statement booklets for the couple, a questions-by-category booklet for the facilitator, and a page of instructions for computer scoring. FOCCUS can also be scored by hand or on a private computer using a Windows® program.

Computer scoring produces a ten-page printout that includes a biographical summary of the couple, a graph of agreement scores for the couple in all topic areas (the twelve content areas, the three summary categories, and any of the three special content areas applicable) and a separate chart of items of agreement and disagreement for each of the topics.

The suggested program for discussing the inventory results is: (1) Discuss reactions to taking the inventory, (2) discuss areas of strong agreement and areas of weak agreement, (3) get the couple to discuss key statements of disagreement, (4) when necessary, teach about a topic the couple has discussed, (5) couple commits to changes. The Facilitator Manual provides summaries of key patterns for couple study for each topic and counselor aids for each of the 189 statements. No specific number of sessions is suggested.

The Premarriage Awareness Inventory

The Premarriage Awareness Inventory (PAI) is actually three inventories: Form F for First Marriage has 119 questions; Form R for Remarriage has 146 questions; and Form C for those who have been Cohabiting for a significant amount of time has 115 questions. The questions in each form address ten topics: Marriage Expectations, Communication, Sharing Feelings, Personality, Conflict Resolution, Family and Friends, Finances, Sexuality, Lifestyle, and Religion.

The PAI program packet contains an Administrator's Portfolio that describes how to do the program; a Counseling packet with two copies each of the participants' forms and one copy each of the scoring booklets for forms F, R, and C; and a forty-six page booklet, *A Good Beginning*, which has short chapters on most of the topics.

The suggested program consists of a first session in which the program is discussed and the inventory completed; second, third, and fourth sessions in which readings from *A Good Beginning* on three or four of the ten topics, with the couple's responses on the inventory, are discussed; and three final sessions in which the particular assigned topics differ for Forms F, R, and C.

Prepare/Enrich Inventory

The *Prepare/Enrich Inventory* (P/E) consists of four inventories: Prepare for childless engaged couples under fifty; Prepare-MC, for engaged couples under fifty with children; Enrich, for married couples under fifty; and Mate, for couples fifty and over preparing to marry, seeking marriage enrichment, or facing other life transitions.

These 165-question inventories cover the following thirteen areas: Idealistic Distortion (tendency to answer questions in a socially desirable manner), Marriage Expectations/Marriage Satisfaction/Life Transitions, Personality, Communication, Conflict Resolution, Finances, Leisure, Sexual Relationship, Children/Intergenerational Issues, Family and Friends/Health Issues, Role Relationship, and

Spiritual Beliefs, plus the Family Map (diagramming couple and family close-ness, and couple and family flexibility).

The P/E program packet consists of a *Counselor's Manual* with: (a) a detailed description of each part of the inventory and program, along with the research that supports it, (b) question booklets and answer sheets for the computer-scored Prepare, Prepare-MC, and Enrich, (c) a twenty-five-page couple's book-let, *Building a Strong Marriage Workbook,* that contains an explanation of the Couple and Family Map along with exercises such as Couple Communication, Assertiveness and Active Listening, Ten Steps for Resolving Conflict, Financial Plans, and Couple Goals.

Within a week after sending the answer sheets for computer scoring, a fifteen-page Counselor report is returned to the pastor. This report includes:

- Background Information (include alcohol/drug abuse, and other abuse)
- Personality Assessment (assertiveness or lack of assertiveness in communi-cation)
- Type of Couple (related to specific relationship and growth areas) and recommendations for working with this couple.
- Item Summary (couple strength and growth areas) Worksheet for Feedback Sessions
- Review of Answers (how each partner answered each question)
- Couple and Family Map describing how each experienced his or her family relationship and how each experience their couple relationship.

The suggested program consists of four sessions: (1) pastor explains the pro-gram, couple contracts for the program and takes the inventory (2) pastor and couple discuss couple's strong areas and growth areas, and pastor assigns a pro-cedure for resolving conflict; (3) pastor reviews the conflict-resolution home-work, couple chooses a new issue to be resolved using the conflict-resolution procedure, pastor explores couple relations or couple's family of origin, and pastor assigns homework on financial plans; (4) pastor and couple review the resolution of the new issue and the financial plans, pastor has the couple com-plete the goal exercise, and pastor reviews the four sessions with the couple.

Comparisons of Inventories

The lack of informative materials on the various topics is the only major weak-ness of FOCCUS and P/E; however, this lack of information must be evaluated in the context of the research that indicates the effectiveness of premarital ques-tionnaires and of relationship teaching (Druckman et al. 1979; Hawley and Olson 1995).

Both PAI and P/E have good programs. They include homework for the cou-ples and an active role for pastors, thus emphasizing the proper contributions of all participants. Each addresses almost all of the recommended topics. They both have clear and full instructions for the pastor or program administrator. FOC-CUS does not have a well-worked-out program or homework for the couple, but it does cover the recommended topics very well.

Significant differences do exist between the premarital inventories. First, PAI leans more toward providing information. The booklet *A Good Beginning* and the coverage of all ten topics in the final three sessions show the emphasis on content. By contrast, P/E emphasizes interaction and couple agreement as illustrated by the contents of *Building a Strong Marriage* and the focus in the sessions on communication, resolving conflict, and the couple and family map. FOCCUS does not provide information or additional exercises; it should be supplemented with *Marriage: A Journey for Life* materials from the same publisher. Second, P/E pays the most attention to the vital topic of family of origin both in its questions and in its feedback program. FOCCUS also highlights the role of family of origin, whereas PAI does not. Third, pastors score the PAI themselves, and the P/E must be sent to its creators to be scored by computer (which gives its authors the data with which to do research). FOCCUS can be scored either way. Finally, the PAI questionnaire and program look adequately put together, but I have not been able to find any research indicating its scientific validity as either an instrument or as a program for helping premarital couples. Both FOCCUS and the P/E questions and program have been conceived, tested, and revised on the basis of solid scientific research (FOCCUS , for example, by Williams and Jurich 1995; P/E, for example, by Larsen and Olsen, 1989).

The major weakness of inventories with feedback sessions when used with individual couples is the absence of a learning community. Premarital inventories are far superior to structured interviews and workbooks, however; research indicates that their use positively correlates with marital happiness. Therefore, I recommend the use of these inventories, preferably with feedback sessions, for use in marriage preparation.

In spite of the expense ($25) and time (a week) required for scoring and returning the P/E, I prefer the P/E because of its emphasis on couple interaction and agreement, its better treatment of family of origin, and the scientific rigor used in developing and revising it. FOCCUS comes a close second to P/E. It has all of P/E's advantages except the well-worked-out program. Its section on the Marriage Covenant covers an area not addressed in P/E. Further, its Religion and Values section seems more relevant to the day-to-day impact of religion on married life than P/E's Spiritual Beliefs section.

COURSES

Courses combine workbooks, leaders, and group interaction into a powerful premarital program. They have the workbook strengths of topic coverage and couple participation, along with the structured interview strength of an active pastor and orderly issue coverage. Courses have the added strengths of a learning community: the empowerment of seeing others in the same situation, the aid of others asking questions that one has but has either not formulated or not asked, opportunities for seeing good communication and conflict-resolution skills modeled, and the chance to get feedback on one's practice of relationship skills. Dyer and Dyer's (1990) *Growing Together* (GT) and Midgley and Midgley's

(1992) *A Decision to Love* (DTL) are two excellent examples of marriage preparation courses.

Both GT and DTL lack the intense pastor-to-couple relationship that individual feedback sessions provide, but the strengths of the learning community more than make up for this weakness for the couple, if not for the pastor. Because GT begins with the taking of a Prepare/Enrich Inventory, it combines the strengths of a course with that of an inventory.

Growing Together

Growing Together builds on the P/E inventories. Couples take an inventory and then use the booklet that describes their results in the discussion of the various topics. Including the inventory-taking session, the program can be done in an eight-week or six-week format. If the inventory is taken two weeks ahead, the program can be done in a weekend format.

In the full eight-week format, the sessions are: (1) Relationship Assessment (introduction and taking the inventory), (2) Family of Origin, (3) Relationship Strengths and Growth Areas, (4) Communication, (5) Managing Anger and Conflict, (6) Intimacy and Sexuality, (7) Financial Management, and (8) Planning for Growth.

Each session of GT, after the first, has five parts: (1) connecting (building community), (2) discovering (where you are), (3) learning (knowledge and skills), (4) contracting (developing a plan of action), and (5) closing (bringing closure). Four specific techniques are used in the sessions: structured exercises, modeling (leaders acting out skills), couple dialogue, and group discussion. The couple's workbook consists primarily of exercises to be done in class or as homework. The session parts and techniques plus the workbook content testify to GT's emphasis on experiential learning and couple interaction and agreement.

A Decision to Love

This marriage preparation program consists of a couple's book and a leader's manual. DTL can be used in courses of various formats, such as an eight-week course, an all-day workshop, or a three-evening format. The leader's manual outlines these formats and suggests a variety of exercises and other ways to present the course material.

The couple's book contains rich resources. Seven meaty chapters each cover one of the following topics: Marriage, Communication/Negotiation, Personalities, Families of Origin, Sexuality, Children, Spirituality, and one combines Finances, Friends, Work, and Leisure. Each of the eight chapters contains a discussion of the topic, separate questionnaires for him and her, discussion questions for partners, and group discussion questions. In addition, the couple's book contains a thirty-five-page wedding liturgy planning guide with an introductory article on planning a wedding, the prayer and Scripture choices for the Roman Catholic liturgy, and two planning sheets.

GT and DTL share much in common; they cover most of the same topics and use sophisticated experiential learning methods. They both lack the intense one-on-couple attention provided by the premarital inventory programs. They differ in that the DTL couple's book contains much more information than the GT couple workbook. In fact, the DTL couple's book can be used by couples as a workbook without a group or a third person, while the GT book cannot. DTL is ecumenical in tone, and, with the exception of the spirituality chapter and the liturgy resources, Roman Catholic teaching is not central. Conversely, GT is non-religious with no spirituality chapter or liturgy resources. The biggest difference between the two is that GT combines the strengths of the Prepare/Enrich inventory with the strengths of a course; because of this difference, I prefer *Growing Together* over *A Decision to Love*.

APPENDIX B

PRAYING THE SERVICE AND SCRIPTURES

Praying the wedding service and Scripture passages at this time is the best way to prepare for praying them on your wedding day. Praying them now will help you understand what the wedding service means and how its message applies to you. Praying the service and Scriptures is also an excellent opportunity to learn to pray together. Lastly, when you grasp how the service and Scriptures speak to your issues, you are better prepared to work with the officiant (and others) in planning your wedding.

To aid your prayer, there are comments on the various parts of "The Celebration and Blessing of a Marriage" and the various suggested passages from Holy Scripture in *Planning Your Marriage Service* (Weber and Weber 1992). The comments briefly state the general meaning of a particular prayer or passage or ceremony.

Your relationship will deepen as you pray together and pray individually. Praying together brings you closer to each other in that you share your particular styles of relating to God and your peculiar insights from God. Praying alone allows you to develop your own type of prayer life and your own comprehension of God's will, which are your gifts to the marriage. Each way of praying depends on the other. Couple prayer depends on the personal relationship with God and the awareness developed in individual prayer. Likewise, individual prayer relies on perceptions and togetherness that flow from couple prayer.

Praying Individually

You can begin praying the service and Scriptures individually by using this simple five-step process:

1. Ask God to open your eyes, heart, and mind so that you can see, feel, and understand what God wants to say to you in this time of prayer.

2. Slowly read over a portion of the service or Scriptures, then slowly read the commentary, and slowly read the portion again.

3. For about five minutes, listen for God's response to you.

4. Make your resolution or response to God's response.

5. Conclude with the Lord's Prayer or the following prayer:

O gracious and everliving God, you have created us male and female in your image: Look mercifully upon *N. and me* who come to you seeking your blessing, and assist us with your grace, that with true fidelity and steadfast love we may honor and keep the promises and vows we make; through Jesus Christ our Savior, who lives and reigns with you in the unity of the Holy Spirit, one God, for ever and ever. Amen. (adapted from *Book of Common Prayer* 1979, 425)

I find it helpful to write notes about this time of prayer in my journal because it helps me to remember what happened. Particularly important to record are the passage prayed over, God's response, and your response to God.

Praying as a Couple

You can pray as a couple by choosing a portion of the service or Scriptures that you want to pray about together, then observing the following six-step process:

1. Each of you pray silently that God will open your eyes, heart, and mind so that you can see, feel, and understand what God wants to say to you through this time of prayer.

2. One of you slowly reads aloud the chosen portion of the service or Scriptures and the commentary. Then the other slowly reads aloud the portion again.

3. After about five minutes of silence, each partner shares a response to the question(s) or reading. It is important that each helps draw out the other's response with questions and paraphrases. Remember, your task is to listen to God speaking through your partner. Therefore, do not argue with your partner's response or use questions to challenge or "improve" her or his response.

4. Each prays silently for a resolution or response to the insight received.

5. Then share the resolution or response with your partner.

6. Conclude by jointly saying the Lord's Prayer or the following prayer:

O gracious and everliving God, you have created us male and female in your image: Look mercifully upon us who come to you seeking your blessing, and assist us with your grace, that with true fidelity and steadfast love we may honor and keep the promises and vows we make; through Jesus Christ our Savior, who lives and reigns with you in the unity of the Holy Spirit, one God, for ever and ever. Amen.

(*Note: The results of your praying and any questions that it raises should be discussed with your pastor.*)

Praying the service and Scriptures takes time and energy, but it is an exciting process of learning more about yourself, your partner, marriage, and God. These understandings are the basis for effective planning of your wedding and for mutual joy in your marriage.

NOTES

2. Skills for Couple Care

1. For a more in-depth discussion of the presence, proclamation, and guidance skills, see *The Skilled Pastor* (Taylor 1991). This discussion differs from that book in two ways: (a) it relates the skills to couple interviews instead of individual conversations, and (b) it groups assessing with proclamation instead of with presence.

3. Session Components and Topics

2. Because assertiveness in communication is so important to marriage, the Prepare 2000 Computer Report has a section that concentrates on this factor.

6. Preparing for the Wedding

3. "Rite for Celebrating Marriage Outside Mass," in *The Rites of the Catholic Church* (New York: Pueblo, 1983), 567–72. "The Celebration and Blessing of a Marriage," in *The Book of Common Prayer* (New York: Seabury, 1997), 422–32. "Marriage," in the *Lutheran Book of Worship* (Minneapolis: Augsburg, 1978), 202–05. "A Service of Christian Marriage I," in *The United Methodist Book of Worship* (Nashville: United Methodist Publishing House, 1992), 115–27; "Christian Marriage: Rite I," in *Book of Common Worship Pastoral Edition* (Presbyterian) (Louisville: Westminster/John Knox, 1993), 111–23; United Church of Christ "Order for Marriage," in the *Book of Worship* (New York: United Church of Christ Office for Church Life and Leadership, 1986), 323–46.

REFERENCES

Anderson, H., and R. C. Fite. 1993. *Becoming married*. Louisville, Ky.: Westminster/John Knox.

Anderson, H., and E. Foley. 1990. A wedding of stories. *New Theological Review* 3:2.

Anderson, H., and K. R. Mitchell. 1993. *Leaving home*. Louisville, Ky.: Westminster/John Knox.

Barth, Markus. 1974. *Ephesians 4–6*. The Anchor Bible. Garden City, N.Y.: Doubleday.

Book of common prayer. 1979. New York: Church Hymnal Corporation and Seabury Press.

Bristow, John Temple. 1988. *What Paul really said about women*. San Francisco: Harper.

Clebsch, W. R., and C. R. Jaekle. 1964. *Pastoral care in historical perspective*. Englewood Cliffs, N. J.: Prentice-Hall.

Clinebell, H. J. 1984. *Basic types of pastoral care and counseling*. Nashville: Abingdon Press.

Clinebell, H. J. 1975. *Growth counseling for marriage enrichment: Premarriage and the early years*. Philadelphia: Fortress Press.

Druckman, J. M., D. G. Fournier, B. Robinson, and D. H. Olson. 1979. *Effectiveness of five types of pre-marital preparation programs*. St. Paul, Minn.: Family Social Science.

Dyer, P., and G. Dyer. 1990. *Growing together*. Minneapolis: Prepare/Enrich Inc.

Egan, G. 1982. *The skilled helper*, 2d ed. Monterey, Calif: Brooks/Cole.

The Episcopal Church. 1991. *Constitution & canons*. New York: General Convention.

Filsinger, E. E., and M. R. Wilson. 1984. Religiosity, socioeconomic rewards, and family development: Predictors of marital adjustment. *Journal of Marriage and the Family* 46: 663–70.

Flowers, B. J., and D. H. Olson. 1986. Predicting marital success with Prepare: A predictive validity study. *Journal of Marital and Family Therapy* 12:403–13.

Friedman, E. H. 1985. *Generation to generation*. New York: Guilford.

Friedman, E. H. 1989. Systems and ceremonies. In *The changing family life cycle*, 2d ed., ed. B. Carter and M. McGoldrick, 119–47. Boston: Allyn and Bacon.

Garland, Diana S. Richmond, and David E. Garland. 1986. *Beyond companionship: Christians in marriage*. Philadelphia: Westminster.

Gottman, J. 1979. *Marital interaction: Empirical investigations*. San Diego: Academic Press.

Gottman, J. 1994. *Why marriages succeed or fail*. New York: Simon & Schuster.

Gottman, J., and L. J. Krokoff. 1989. "Marital interaction and satisfaction: A longitudinal view." *Journal of Consulting and Clinical Psychology* 57:47–52.

Gray, J. 1992. *Men are from Mars, women are from Venus.* New York: Harper-Collins.

Greeley, A. 1991. *Faithful attraction.* New York: Tom Doherty Associates Inc.

Greeley, A. M. 1980. *The young Catholic family: Religious images and marriage fulfillment.* Chicago: Thomas More.

Grenz, L. and D. Glover. 1996. *The marriage journey.* Boston: Cowley.

Hauk, P. 1972. *Reason in pastoral counseling.* Philadelphia: Westminster.

Hawley, D. R., and D. H. Olson. 1995. Enriching newlyweds: An evaluation of three marital enrichment programs with newlywed couples. *The American Journal of Family Therapy* 23, 2, 129–47.

Hendrix, H. 1988. *Getting the love you want.* Perennial Library, 1990 ed. New York: Harper.

Hines, P. M., and N. Boyd-Franklin. 1982. Black families. In *Ethnicity and family therapy,* ed. M. McGoldrick, 84–107. New York: Guilford.

Hunt, J. and R. Hunt. 1982. *Preparing for Christian marriage.* Nashville: Abingdon.

Jewett, P. K. 1975. *Man as male and female.* Grand Rapids: Eerdmans.

Jerusalem Bible, the. 1966. Garden City, N.Y.: Doubleday.

Larsen, A. S. and D. H. Olson. 1989. Predicting marital satisfaction using Prepare: A replication study. *Journal of Marital and Family Therapy,* 15: 311–22.

Markey, B., M. Micheletto, and A. Becker. 1997. FOCCUS, 2d ed. FOCCUS, Inc.; Omaha, Neb.: Family Life Office of Omaha.

Markman, H. J., F. J. Floyd, S. M. Stanley, and R. D. Storaasli. 1988. "Prevention of marital distress: A longitudinal investigation." *Journal of Consulting and Clinical Psychology* 56:210–17.

Markman, H. J., M. J. Renick, F. J. Floyd, S. M. Stanley, and M. Clements. 1993. "Preventing marital distress through communication and conflict management training: A 4- and 5-year follow-up." *Journal of Consulting and Clinical Psychology* 61:1–80.

Markman, H. J., S. M. Stanley, and S. L. Blumberg. 1994. *Fighting for your marriage.* San Francisco: Jossey-Bass Publishers.

Martos, J. 1993. Marriage. In *Perspectives on marriage,* ed. K. Scott and M. Warren, 30–68. New York: Oxford.

Midgley, J. M. V. and S. V. Midgley. 1992. *A decision to love.* Mystic, Conn.: Twenty-Third Publications.

Mittman, J. L. C. 1980. *Premarital counseling.* New York: Seabury.

Olson, D. H. 1996. *Prepare/Enrich counselor's manual.* Minneapolis: Prepare/Enrich.

Olthoff, C. 1989. The effectiveness of premarital communication training. Ph.D. diss., California Graduate School of Family Psychology, San Rafael, Calif.

Phillips, J. B. 1972. *The New Testament in modern English,* rev. ed. New York: MacMillan.

Rotunno, M., and M. McGoldrick. 1982. Italian families. In *Ethnicity and family therapy,* ed. M. McGoldrick, 340–63. New York: Guilford.

Scanzoni, L. and N. Hardesty. 1974. *All we're meant to be*. Waco, Tex.: Word.

Schaller, L. E. 1988. *44 ways to increase church attendance*. Nashville: Abingdon.

Stahmann, R. F., and W. J. Hiebert. 1987. *Premarital counseling*, 2d ed. Lexington, Mass.: D. C. Heath.

Taylor, C. W. 1991. *The skilled pastor*. Minneapolis: Fortress Press.

Velander, Peter L. 1993. *The premarriage awareness inventory*. Inver Grove Heights, Minn.: Logos.

Weber, C. L. and M. Weber. 1992 *Planning your marriage service*. Harrisburg, Pa.: Morehouse.

Williams, L., and J. Jurich. 1995. "Predicting marital success after five years: Assessing the predictive validity of FOCCUS," *Journal of Marital and Family Therapy* 21:141–53.